Strategic Market Research

A Guide to Conducting Research that Drives Businesses

By

Anne E. Beall, PhD
President, Beall Research & Training, Inc.

iUniverse, Inc.
New York   Bloomington

Strategic Market Research
A Guide to Conducting Research that Drives Businesses

Copyright © 2010 by Beall Research & Training, Inc.

iUniverse Star
an iUniverse, Inc. imprint

iUniverse books may be ordered through booksellers or by contacting:

iUniverse
1663 Liberty Drive
Bloomington, IN 47403
www.iuniverse.com
1-800-Authors (1-800-288-4677)

ISBN: 978-1-936236-16-9 (pbk)
ISBN: 978-1-936236-17-6 (ebk)

Library of Congress Control Number: 2010908947

Printed in the United States of America

iUniverse Rev. Date 6/30/2010

All images in this book are used by permission of Shutterstock.com.

Also by Anne Beall

The Psychology of Gender

Reading the Hidden Communications Around You

For Doug, Michael, and Kelsey

Contents

Preface

Ever since I was a child, I've been fascinated by people. This fascination led me to study psychology in college and eventually to earn a PhD in social psychology from Yale University. While I was in graduate school, I became increasingly frustrated with the academic path that lay in front of me. I had been trained to be an academic researcher and to teach college students, but I wanted to do more. I wanted to go into the "real world" and use my skills to help organizations. I wanted to make a difference. My path led me to a career in market research, which is the study of how people think about and relate to brands, products, and services. When market research is done well, it helps companies respond intelligently to their markets and to offer products and services that people actually want and need. Through market research, companies have introduced many of the products and services that make our lives better.

In the fifteen years that I've been conducting market research, I've learned about many different businesses, worked on a variety of intellectually challenging problems, and seen the results of my research in the real world. I've seen new products launched that I was intimately involved with from the start, and I've watched ad campaigns that I initially tested. I've seen people use products that would have never been designed if our research had not been conducted. I've seen companies become stronger and create more jobs as a result of how effectively they compete in their markets. I know that many of the products and services that we've researched have made a difference for the people who buy them.

It is my passion for my work that drove me to write this book. I believe in market research, and I want to give back to the industry that provided me with a way to make a living and the chance to make a difference. I wrote this book for people who buy or use market research and for those who conduct it. Some might say that it's not in my self-interest to share my approach with competitors, but I disagree. The better our industry becomes, the more we grow, and the more value we will provide to our clients. Many companies use market research. This book applies equally to for-profit businesses and nonprofit organizations. We work with many different types of organizations, and I give many examples of these projects throughout this book.

I hope that you enjoy reading this book as much as I've enjoyed writing it.

Acknowledgments

There are many people who have helped me in my career and who have contributed greatly to the content of this book. My mentors at National Analysts in Philadelphia taught me the basics of good market research and how to take research to a deeper, more consultative level. The group that I worked with at The Boston Consulting Group (BCG) believed in market research and showed me how it could be used to drive the major strategies for an organization. While I was at BCG, my fellow researchers and I honed our skills in the area of interviewing, and I began to develop my thinking on reading nonverbal communication.

I want to thank the many clients I've worked with over the years and particularly since I began my company, Beall Research & Training. My clients have pushed me as much as I've pushed them, and our partnership has been extraordinary. Many of the people I've worked with have suggested new ways of looking at things or different ways to approach problems and have taken our research results and created large changes in their organizations. You are my heroes.

I also want to thank the many people who work with me on a regular basis and who recruit for my studies, tabulate my data, and help me moderate interviews and focus groups. I want particularly to thank Nancy Anthony, Kevin Rooney, Peter Csizmadia, Michael Taylor, and Mindy Predovic.

Another group of people to whom I'm indebted are the respondents who have participated in my many projects. Because of your honesty and ability to share your thoughts and feelings, I have been able to garner tremendous insights.

Last, I want to thank my husband, Doug Doolittle, and my children, Michael and Kelsey Doolittle. You have been very patient with me during this writing process, and I appreciate all your support. I dedicate this book to you.

1

What's Wrong with Traditional Market Research?

Market research is a multibillion dollar industry that grows every year. Since 1988, spending on market research has typically grown about 8 percent a year. Growth rates have varied from a low of 4 percent in 2002 to a high of 13 percent in 1997 (Honomichl 2007). In 2006, spending on market research was approximately $8.1 billion (Honomichl 2007). That's a lot of money. Even without these statistics, you can sense how much market research is growing when you see the proliferation of offers to become a research participant. One recent ad that I saw suggested that you can make thousands of dollars by being a research respondent *full-time*!

Yet with all this spending on market research, I seem to hear more complaints. Research buyers at major companies that spend thousands of dollars on market research don't always feel that they get the best value for their money; they don't get tremendous insights, and they don't acquire information that helps them make strategic decisions for their businesses. In short, they often have a lot of information, but not many answers. Another complaint is that buyers sometimes feel that market research provides them with information that is so superficial that it tells them what they already know. The last complaint is that it examines an issue in a way that provides erroneous information and leads to poor business decisions. So what is the problem?

Some critics of traditional market research say the techniques are to blame. They point out that focus groups can unduly influence research participants and cause respondents to espouse opinions that they do not really hold. Other critics claim that traditional market research does not fully capture the emotions of participants and tends to put forward a rational explanation for human behavior, which is complex and due to a combination of reason and emotion. Generally, those who are highly critical of traditional market research techniques are trying to sell their specific research technique, which coincidentally doesn't have any of the problems they mention.

Other critics claim that it's the specific suppliers of market research who are to blame. Often the more strategic thinkers sell the market research study, and then the project managers and people who execute the work lose their way. What may seem like such a clear project in the beginning can evolve into a myriad of questions and a set of data that doesn't really say anything in the end. Clients who are savvy in purchasing market research sometimes become allied with specific individuals in supplier organizations whom they believe can deliver for them. However, most individuals cannot be all things to all clients, so when techniques or questions change, this alliance may not be useful.

As someone who has been in market research since 1993, I don't believe that the problem is the techniques or the people. I've designed and executed hundreds of studies—both qualitative and quantitative—moderated hundreds of focus groups, conducted thousands of individual interviews, and fielded hundreds of surveys. I've also bought market research from top suppliers in the industry. Having seen the industry from both sides of the table, my observation is that the problem is how market research is designed, executed, and analyzed. Much market research comprises the gathering of information for the sake of gathering it. It's not inspired, and it doesn't drive businesses to make decisions that will help them to compete.

I want to share my approach to conducting market research. My background combines academic training with real-world consulting. After completing my PhD at Yale University, I was hired by a consulting firm that taught academic researchers how to conduct business research. I eventually worked at the Boston Consulting Group, a major management consulting firm, where I directed market research for its Chicago office. I now have my own firm, Beall Research & Training, Inc. All of the research that I conduct is strategic in nature. Our research is different than much market research in terms of how we design it, how we obtain insight from respondents, and how we interpret what we learn. The purpose of this book is to share our approach.

The Strategic Approach

The strategic approach to market research uses a set of principles that are invaluable in our work. These principles are:

- •Identifying the strategic questions that will help a business
- •Using the right research techniques to answer these questions
- •Obtaining the level of depth required to have insight
- •Reading the nonverbal communications of research respondents when doing qualitative work
- •Identifying the emotional aspects of human behavior
- •Using statistical analyses to understand what drives markets
- •Going beyond the data to interpret the results and make strategic recommendations

My experience is that good research projects include all of the above. In cases where the research breaks down, it's because one of the principles above is violated. These principles are relevant regardless of the organization that is commissioning the research. It doesn't matter if the organization is a Fortune 100 company or a small nonprofit association in the community.

How This Book Is Organized

I discuss each of these research principles in the following chapters. Each chapter builds on the previous one to show how the principles work together. Within each chapter, I highlight real examples of how I've used each principle to my advantage.

- •**Chapter 2** is about the strategic question-based approach to market research, which is the foundation for designing a good project.
- •**Chapter 3** is about how to select the correct method. I discuss both qualitative and quantitative methods, explaining the tradeoffs of each major research method.
- •**Chapter 4** is about how to get the depth needed to gain useful insights that answer a strategic question.
- •**Chapter 5** is about how to read the nonverbal communications of research respondents. Often these nonverbal behaviors tell us volumes about what people think and feel.

•**Chapter 6** is about how to get to the heart of respondents' emotions and determine the role emotions play in perceptions and behaviors.

•**Chapter 7** discusses statistical analyses and ways they can be used in quantitative work to understand what drives a market.

•**Chapter 8** is about interpreting findings from a market research study; it provides guidelines for how to go beyond the data to help an organization.

•**Chapter 9** is about some of the common pitfalls that occur in market research. I've seen all of them, and they're easy to avoid if you know about them in advance.

2

The Strategic-Question
Approach to Market
Research

If there is one thing that can make the difference between excellent and poor market research, it's the nature of the question that is being asked. My experience is that the best projects tend to be ones in which a very specific question with strategic significance for an organization is answered. Unfortunately, many research projects tend to have a myriad of vague questions that the organization wants to answer. Often the result of all these questions is a long discussion guide in the case of qualitative research or a long survey in the case of quantitative work. This approach tends to reveal a large amount of information across a variety of topics, but it tends to have little depth.

I once did some work for a dental-supply company that did very little research about its customers. Its customers were dentists all over the country. Because the company did so little market research, the client wanted to know almost everything about the customers. The company wanted to know how dentists viewed their products, how they made decisions, how often they saw representatives from competitors, what they regarded as the strengths and weaknesses of the company's products, and so on. The list was endless. We ended up with a long discussion guide for individual interviews with dentists all over the country At the end of this study, we knew a little about a lot of things. The client was disappointed. He claimed that he already knew much of what we had learned and that he had gained few strategic insights about what to do with his company. That experience was a valuable lesson for me.

What I learned was that trying to answer many questions is often less valuable than answering one or two major ones that are important to an organization. With one or two questions, I can obtain the depth required to really answer the questions and provide sound recommendations as a result. I like to compare the dental-supply company with a nonprofit association that approached me about doing market research to determine if it would make sense to change its name. The question was clear and straightforward. Some of their members were advocating a name change because they thought the name was old-fashioned and gave an inaccurate perception of the association. I suggested interviewing members about their perceptions of the association, their perceptions of the name, whether they thought the name should be changed, and if so, what a new name should convey. The results of this research indicated that the association should keep its name but should change its logo and marketing materials. The clients were pleased with the study because it gave them clear answers to a major question, and it provided strategic direction for them.

So clearly having a few good questions is preferable to having a myriad of questions. Sometimes, though, one question can be a poor question. Whenever clients approach me about doing research for them, I always ask what their objective is in conducting this work. On many occasions people will tell me that their company wants to "understand our customers better," "figure out what's important to customers," or "identify how to sell more of our products and services." All of these questions are very vague, and they presume a number of questions underneath each one. "Understanding our customers better" is not an objective that can be clearly translated into a market research project. Every organization wants to understand its customers or clients. It's the specifics of what an organization wants to understand that form the basis of a good question.

Assessing Research Questions

So what makes a good question? A good question is very specific about what should be learned from a research project. When a good question is answered, it provides a clear direction for the organization. A good way to assess potential research questions is to use the following evaluation criteria:

- Is there a clear strategic question that the organization needs to answer?

6

- Is this one specific question or a conglomeration of questions? For example, "What is important to customers?" is actually several questions disguised as one question. In contrast, "How important is price when purchasing this product?" is one question.

• Are there *specific* questions that need to be answered in order to address this strategic question?

- For example, "How much does price play a factor in the purchase of *X*?" and "What is the price elasticity for product *Y*?" are specific questions that might need to be answered to address a specific strategic question.

• Is there a current hypothesis about the answer to this question?

- Are there current beliefs about what we will learn when we conduct this study?

• If the organization knew this information, would they take specific actions as a result?

- If the organization knew this information, what strategic actions would they take because of this information?

If you can answer "yes" to all the criteria above, then you have an excellent question. See Table 1 for some examples of good and poor research questions.

In many cases, organizations do not approach us with excellent questions. Our job is to help them think through their objectives and to arrive at good questions that will turn into good research designs. We strive to meet the criteria discussed above. In situations where clients have a vague question or a conglomeration of questions, we help them to identify the strategic question. The approach that we use is to ask them a series of questions that will illuminate the major issues. We will ask questions such as:

• What is the major objective of this study?

• Which person or department is driving this research?

• What is the reason they want to conduct research?

• Is there a current issue or problem that is motivating the commission of this research?

• What are some of the *specific* things your organization wants to understand?

7

- If you had to prioritize the set of things you want to know, what are the first, second, and third things you would want to learn?

We have found that, as clients begin to think about these questions, their vague, conglomerated questions become clearer. A set of questions becomes one strategic question with several specific subquestions that will help us answer that major question.

For example, clients may say that they want to understand their customers better so they can sell more of their housecleaning services. After a discussion, we may find that they had placed ads in newspapers to try to win new customers. These ads did not bring in new business, and they want to understand why. The question of "How do we sell more housecleaning services?" has illuminated the following questions: 1) Do people use ads to find housecleaning services? 2) If they do use ads, what was the problem with these recent ads—why didn't they work? 3) If people do not use ads, how do they find housecleaning services? 4) What are the criteria people use in evaluating potential housecleaning services—in other words, what do people want to know before they will call to inquire about a housecleaning service? Thus, the strategic question is "What medium and what communications should we use to win new customers?" The specific questions that were just outlined fall under this strategic query.

One of the ways I learn about the important questions of a project is to ask what the current hypotheses are before we begin a study. Hypotheses are the current thoughts about the results of a study—what clients think we may learn. Generally, if there is a hypothesis, there is a specific question. Thus, by asking what people in the organization currently believe, we are elucidating the issues that clients are discussing and for which they will ultimately want answers in order to do their jobs. We typically ask:

- What do people believe we will learn when we conduct this research?

- What are the current thoughts in the organization about what is happening in the market with regard to this issue?

- What are the reasons people have these hypotheses?

By understanding the hypotheses that our clients hold, we will specifically know the things that they will want to test and what particular answers they are seeking to prove or disprove. For example, with our housecleaning service, the client may believe that people don't use ads to find house cleaners and that they typically ask friends for referrals. Or this client may hypothesize that people use ads but that the recent ad wasn't effective because it failed to provide important information.

After defining the major questions for an organization, we always ask how they would use the information. We ask:

- •What would the organization do if it knew this information?
- •What specific decisions would the organization make in response to this research?
- •What can the organization realistically change or do in response to this project?

This information is critical to understanding some of the specifics of what organizations need to know. In the housecleaning example, we might learn that as a result of this project this business will determine which marketing vehicles to use and how much money to allocate. In this case, we would want to understand what newspapers and other periodicals these customers peruse when looking for house cleaners. This business might also want to know what was positive or negative about the recent ad it placed. For this project, we would want potential customers to look at the ad and tell us what the ad conveys to them and the major reasons they would or would not call in response to it.

When you go through this process and help people to re-frame their research questions, what begins as one type of project can evolve into a totally different one. Recently I worked with a large organization that provides educational materials to instructors all over the country. It had changed some of its materials, and wanted to have instructors review all of these changes and give them feedback. I reviewed the materials and could not see major differences from their earlier ones. I asked the clients what they ultimately wanted to accomplish; they explained that they believed the materials were improved and they wanted to make sure instructors would not reject them. Our project changed from a question about how instructors feel about all the different changes to one in which the strategic question was "How do we communicate the changes in our materials to the instructors?" The specific questions that we needed to answer were: 1) Do instructors notice the changes and, if they do, which ones do they notice? 2) How do they feel about these changes—are they perceived as improvements or not? 3) What do instructors want to know about these changes in order to feel positively about them? In other words, what justification do they need to understand these changes? Because we reframed the question, we ended up providing a great deal of value to this organization. We turned a somewhat trivial project into one where the information was used to create a communication strategy for the new course materials.

Poor Question	Good Question
What is important to customers?	What specific needs does this product or service fulfill?
How is our product perceived compared to those of competitors?	How do customers perceive the features of our product compared to the features of our competitor's product? Is the major feature that differentiates our product from the competition valued by customers? Would this product replace usage of other similar products in the marketplace?
How do customers make decisions when purchasing this service?	What are the key criteria that people use when selecting this service? What 2–3 criteria are the most important?
What do customers think about this potential new product?	How likely would customers be to purchase this product as it is currently envisioned?
What do customers think about this new service?	What do customers specifically like and dislike about this service? What are the unmet needs this service would fulfill?

Table 1: Examples of Good and Poor Research Questions

3

Choosing the Right Method

All research methods have positive and negative aspects to them, and there are many ways to conduct a study. There are numerous ways to answer a question, and different techniques each offer something positive and negative. Market researchers sometimes criticize one another for using specific techniques, pointing out the weaknesses of competitors' techniques while espousing the strengths of their own. I always find these conversations amusing because all of us in the industry know that game. Generally, with qualitative research, an excellent moderator who is using a research technique that she is comfortable using will end up providing useful information. In quantitative research, a well-worded survey that is thoughtful and covers the major issues will deliver tremendous value. In many cases the shortcomings of research tend to be the result of not taking a strategic-question approach to the problem and not understanding the issues that are important to the organization, which was just discussed in chapter 2.

In this chapter I talk about the major market-research techniques that are available and some of the tradeoffs of using each one. The objective of this discussion is to acquaint you with some excellent uses for each technique and some of the pitfalls of each approach. It is not meant to be an exhaustive summary of every potential methodology with all possible pros and cons. However, before considering each technique, one has to decide whether to conduct qualitative or quantitative research.

Qualitative or Quantitative Research?

Qualitative research comprises research techniques in which you gather qualitative information—general thoughts, feelings, usage patterns, and so on. Examples of these techniques include focus groups, individual interviews, and observations of product usage. Quantitative research comprises techniques in which you gather numeric data of some type and the sample sizes are large enough to do statistical analyses. Sample sizes can range from one hundred to thousands of respondents. Examples of these techniques include Internet surveys, mail surveys, and in-person intercept surveys.

So when do you do qualitative versus quantitative research? The straightforward answer is that when you want to collect numeric data, quantitative research is the way to go. This answer is not necessarily correct. Often people don't know what kind of data they need and having information in numeric form isn't as important as having good answers. Typically, we suggest doing qualitative research if little or no work has been done on the topic and if the project is somewhat exploratory. We generally recommend conducting qualitative research before doing any quantitative work. Qualitative work allows us to explore all the potential thoughts, feelings, and behaviors of a particular group of people. It's only when we understand all of these things that we can confidently measure them in a survey of this same group. Qualitative work also provides us with an opportunity to generate additional hypotheses that we can test in quantitative work. Thus, our quantitative work is well-informed by our qualitative work.

Qualitative research is generally ideal when:

- Little or no research has been conducted on this topic
- The objective of this research is somewhat exploratory
- There is a need to explore some issues in depth to understand thoughts, feelings, and behaviors
- There is some uncertainty about the issues that may be influencing behavior

Quantitative research is generally ideal when:

- Qualitative research has already been conducted on this topic
- The major thoughts, feelings, and behaviors have been illuminated among this customer group
- The objective is to measure specific thoughts, feelings, and behaviors among a broader set of people

•There is a need to have numeric quantification of these thoughts, feelings, and behaviors

Qualitative Methods

There are numerous qualitative techniques that can be used. We now explore some of the most commonly used ones and their major advantages and disadvantages.

Focus Groups, Minigroups, and Triads

Focus groups, which are group discussions moderated by a facilitator, are one of the most commonly used qualitative methods. This method may even be overused by researchers. The major advantage of this technique is that you can hear from numerous people in a small amount of time when you use a group to understand some aspect of the market. You get a broad overview of thoughts, feelings, and behaviors particularly if you talk with many different types of people. Another advantage is that you can use the group dynamic to explore issues in a way that would be more difficult with an individual. The major disadvantage of focus groups is that the group dynamic can sometimes get in the way of collecting accurate thoughts and feelings from people. I will discuss some of the pros and cons of this approach.

The major advantage of focus groups is that you can use the group dynamic to unearth things that are difficult to obtain from individuals. Groups can create an atmosphere of trust, disclosure, and an easy interchange of ideas. For example, some of the work that we do is for clinical trials. All medications must be tested in clinical trials to be approved by the FDA. Organizations that run clinical trials want to understand what would motivate people to participate in these trials so they can communicate effectively with these groups. People have different reasons for wanting to participate in a clinical trial. Some want to make a contribution to the world, and others want to try a new treatment because they're dissatisfied with their current one. These conversations can be very emotional. It's often difficult for one person to articulate some of these deep-seated feelings and what their participation might mean to them. Usually one person begins to explain these feelings, and another one will expand on these thoughts and further articulate them. Other group members will begin to add their thoughts to the subject, and as a result of this group process, we will understand something that is complicated.

The group setting also allows members to stimulate one another's thinking in the interaction. I use focus groups to generate broad lists of thoughts, feelings, and behaviors. For example, in work for a retail store, we generated all the words that come to mind when people hear that store's name. Respondents said the words that came to mind, and these words sparked new words in response. The list became long, and several key themes emerged. These themes were then analyzed to describe this retail brand. We also do similar exercises with respondents about all the major uses they have for a particular product—the reasons they use the product and when they tend to use it. Getting ideas for all of these uses helps us determine when and why things are used. We also use focus groups to generate creative ideas. Sometimes we use creative consumers—people who are particularly creative—or sometimes we just have respondents think about all the unique ways to use or think about something.

All is not rosy with focus groups, however. Sometimes people are unduly influenced by other respondents, particularly ones with dominant personalities. If a moderator does not maintain control of the discussion, a respondent with a strong personality can take over a group, and it can become the venue for hearing only one opinion. At the end of the group, one is unsure what the other respondents were actually thinking. Another problem is that people may be less likely to divulge what they really think and do in a group because they are actively managing the impression they give to others in this setting. The result could be a focus group in which people are telling you what they think they should say rather than telling you what they actually do or think. These criticisms are all valid. Expert moderators generally have ways of creating an atmosphere for honest disclosure and have ways of handling these types of problems. We also have ways of judging whether people are actively managing how they come across rather than revealing what's really going on in their lives.

One of the major issues with focus groups is something called *group polarization*. Interestingly, groups tend to intensify their members' opinions if they all share a particular viewpoint. Thus, if all the people in a focus group tend to be positively predisposed toward a particular politician before the discussion, they will be even more positive about this person after it. Apparently the group members reinforce one another's ideas and encourage stronger attitudes. This effect has been found in numerous research studies across many different people (Myers 2002). Group polarization can have a tremendous impact on how you interpret focus group findings because you can misread a group's enthusiasm for or aversion to a product. You may believe that this product will be a hit (or a tremendous bomb) if you don't factor in the polarization effect. Good moderators have ways of creating dissension in groups and encouraging other viewpoints to address this effect. However, group polarization is sometimes inevitable.

Over the course of fifteen years, I have become increasingly enamored of minigroups (four to five people per group) and triads (three people per group). These types of focus groups allow for a greater degree of depth with each person than the traditional eight- to ten-person group, and they allow me to encourage intimate disclosures. This method is one that I've become very comfortable using because it balances breadth and depth using the group dynamic. However, as I mentioned earlier, there is not one correct method—just different options that have their tradeoffs.

Individual Interviews—In the Home, at Work, or in a Facility

Individual interviews, as the name implies, involve talking to only one person. Thus, projects with individual interviews tend to involve fewer total respondents than focus-group projects. However, these interviews allow us to explore individual motivations and behaviors in great detail and to piece together the various influences on behavior. We use these interviews to elicit what is important in the abstract and then to have people give us stories of their experiences buying or using a product or service. These stories often tell us about all the actual influences on behavior, and we can analyze these stories to see if there are common themes. We can also compare these stories to the abstract reasons that people give us about what's important to them. Sometimes what people say is important is not actually borne out in their examples. For example, in some individual interviews that we did with consumers, they told us that price is an important factor in their decision to purchase household goods. However, their stories told us otherwise.

Where we conduct individual interviews varies. We prefer to go to people's homes or workplaces if we believe that understanding these environments is important for that product or service. Respondents' homes and workplaces can reveal important aspects about how they live and work. These environments can also reveal what is important to people. In a recent project for an apparel company, we went to teens' homes to understand the clothing that is important to them and to see how clothing creates part of their identity. We asked teens to bring out some of their favorite clothing so we could take a look at what constituted a favorite clothing piece. Some of the teens took us into their rooms to get their clothing, and we were able to see how these teenagers arranged their spaces, what they put on their walls, and how they defined themselves. We gained much more insight about these teens as a result of using this method. We also use this method if we have trouble getting respondents to come to a facility. For example, when we interview executives, we sometimes have difficulty getting them to come to our locations, so we go to their workplaces.

The major drawback of individual interviews is the amount of time one needs to conduct them. Our interviews are typically an hour long; when we do in-home or at-work interviews, the amount of time we expend on travel and interviewing can be as much as three hours for each person. In cases where we don't believe that going to someone's home or workplace is useful, we will do individual interviews in a facility. Another drawback is that these interviews involve so much depth with each person that one can sometimes feel, at the end of ten interviews, that there are ten different stories but no particular pattern in the results. As a result, we tend to do ten interviews for each customer group, and then we analyze the group of interviews for consistent patterns.

In-Depth Telephone Interviews

In situations where we're interviewing a small number of people who are spread across a wide geography, it makes sense to do an in-depth telephone interview. For example, some of the studies we conduct are with investigators who conduct large clinical trials. These investigators are high-level physicians. Sometimes we only have fifteen investigators who are located all over the United States. Even if we could interview them in a facility or at their workplaces, they have a tendency to be very busy and to cancel appointments at the last minute. In these situations it makes sense to conduct an in-depth telephone interview; we can schedule it at the investigators' convenience, we don't need to travel to fifteen different cities, and, if participants cancel at the last minute, we haven't absorbed huge travel costs.

In addition to these obvious advantages, in-depth telephone interviews can be very useful for sensitive subjects that people may be uncomfortable discussing in person. I have a colleague who only does in-depth telephone interviews because he's convinced that people disclose more over the telephone with him than when they are with him in person. I think it depends on the topic that you're discussing. If you're talking about something that's highly personal and would benefit from the anonymity of the telephone, it can be a very useful method. However, if you set the right atmosphere for disclosure, an in-person interview can accomplish the same things as a telephone interview.

One disadvantage of this method is the limited time that people want to talk on the telephone. Most people don't like to hold a telephone to their ear for more than twenty or thirty minutes, so you generally can't do a one-hour interview like you can with an in-person method. The other disadvantage is that people have a tendency to multitask while you are interviewing them. People answer e-mails, surf the Internet, and occasionally eat during interviews. Obviously, you don't always have respondents' full attention. The other problem with this method is that you cannot see the people you're interviewing, which means that a whole host of nonverbal cues are unavailable to you. I talk about reading the hidden communications of research respondents and the type of information you can glean from people by their body language in an upcoming chapter.

Shop-Alongs

Shop-alongs are literally shopping trips that we make with respondents to stores where they normally shop. We use this method when we want to understand the effect that a retail environment has on a person. Respondents will tend to tell you to the best of their knowledge how stores influence their behavior, but often they don't really know how they shop in stores and what induces them to buy certain items. Because we cannot expect human beings to have perfect insight into themselves, we try to understand how retail environments and sales associates influence them by going shopping with them and observing for ourselves.

When I first started my business, I received a call from a major manufacturing company that wanted to do focus groups to understand what is important to consumers when buying its product. For client confidentiality reasons, let's say it was a company that manufactures televisions. I had a hunch that people didn't always know what they want when it comes to this product because it was a fairly infrequent purchase, and I suspected that the retail environment has a large influence on shopper behavior. I recommended doing shop-alongs to ascertain the impact of the store on customers. They were a little leery about this technique, but were intrigued and we started doing shop-alongs. The results were very illuminating. Customers were tremendously influenced by the salespeople and by the environment in which they were shopping. Often they would walk in with a certain brand and specific product in mind and then would buy something completely different. They changed their minds because the sales associate would educate them about new technology or encourage them to buy a different product and brand. The results helped to change how salespeople were trained and how this product was sold in major stores.

I am a tremendous proponent of shop-alongs, but only when you need to understand how stores influence customers and when you want to learn how customers shop for certain products. Shop-alongs, however, are not a great source for insight about why products are preferred or how people use them. Typically the output of shop-alongs is an overview of the shopping process and what is effective or ineffective in a retail environment for a particular category. The major disadvantage of this method is that it can be time-consuming and the researcher's presence can sometimes alter the respondent's behavior. We try, however, to create as normal an interaction as possible and have gleaned a tremendous amount of insight from this technique.

Observation

Another useful method is observation. We have learned a great deal from just watching customers use things that they buy. In a study that I did for a food manufacturer, I observed how people store and prepare food when they have young children. I learned that often what people tell you about their desire for nutritious foods is not borne out when you look at the foods they cook and serve. When you look at what they buy and store in their pantries, you get a better understanding of what really matters. Although mothers will say that they only care about serving their children nutritious food, it appears that getting young children to eat and having as little fuss as possible at the table may be more important.

Sometimes before doing qualitative research on a topic, I will observe as many people as possible to understand customer behavior. In a study that I did on greeting cards, I spent time watching people shop for greeting cards at local stores. I noticed that there were several segments of greeting card shoppers and that they approached the cards quite differently. As a result of watching people closely, I could see that there was clearly a group that was highly involved with the category, and they enjoyed the selection process. At the other end of the spectrum were people who wanted to pick up a card as quickly as possible and get out. There were several other segments in between. Knowing these segments helped me to understand how to structure the qualitative research and to sample each of these groups.

Online Discussion Forums and Focus Groups

As our communication becomes more reliant on electronic media, online focus groups and discussion forums are techniques that are being embraced by the research community. These two techniques involve a moderator posting a question and respondents posting their answers online. The focus group is a two-hour session, whereas the discussion forum occurs over the course of several days, and respondents log into the session when it's convenient for them.

We have successfully used online discussion forums and focus groups in several situations. We have found they're useful when the respondents are not close enough geographically to have a focus group. We have also found them useful when we want to have a discussion among a national sample of people. For example, we did a study with instructors who were located all over the country. There were not enough of them in several geographic locations to conduct the number of focus groups that we wanted, so we did an online discussion forum with people all across the United States. We then did two to three focus groups in two major cities where there were enough people to recruit in-person focus groups.

One advantage of these methods is that sometimes people feel more comfortable interacting online than they do in person. Younger respondents tend to be particularly comfortable communicating in this way because they spend a lot of time interacting in chat rooms, over Web sites, and through text messages. Older respondents may find this anonymity particularly comfortable, especially if they are discussing highly personal or embarrassing topics. One of my colleagues just did a study in which she was discussing female sanitary supplies with women. The online discussion forum proved to be the perfect method for having this sensitive discussion.

The major disadvantage of these techniques is that they do not occur in person, so you cannot observe respondents' nonverbal communication and see how they are responding. Even worse than not being able to see respondents' body language is the possibility that respondents can lie in an online environment and pretend to be someone they are not. Electronic communications offer people the opportunity to role play and to assume identities that are not real. There is often no way to tell if that is happening.

Quantitative Research Techniques

In this section I discuss some of the major quantitative techniques and their principal advantages and disadvantages. This section could be an entire book itself. Quantitative research can be complicated when one takes into account sampling, weighting of respondent data, and analysis of the results. These topics are beyond the scope of this book and are discussed by authors who specialize in these areas.

However, it is important to stress that when selecting a quantitative method, the final sample of respondents must represent a specific population. If the data does not represent that group accurately, it is worthless. Thus, the sampling frame is an extremely important part of evaluating each method. You want to think about who would participate in this type of quantitative research and why. In addition, you want to have specific quotas for age, gender, region, and income, depending on the nature of the product or service. Just launching an Internet survey among a random group of people is a practice that I abhor because it can lead to spurious results. In studies where we are trying to represent an entire state, region, or country, we will determine after the data is collected if we have met our quotas for each group. If we have not, we will weight the data so that it represents the population exactly.

Internet Surveys

Internet surveys are one of my favorite methods because so many people are online, and they're used to answering questions over the Internet. In addition, the online population is fairly representative of the total population, particularly in North America. We have successfully conducted numerous Internet studies on a variety of topics—everything from GPS navigational systems to flooring purchases. The major advantage of this method is that it allows researchers the opportunity to program skip patterns into questionnaires to explore specific issues in detail. Thus, if respondents say that they have a Toshiba computer, we can ask specific questions that relate only to Toshiba. Those who purchased their computer online would be asked a series of questions about how they decided to purchase their computer and what the advantages and disadvantages of buying online are.

Another advantage of doing Internet surveys is that one can survey low-incidence populations—groups of consumers that are only 1 to 5 percent of the population. As a result, Internet surveys are more affordable and less time-consuming than techniques such as telephone surveys. If we have to make one hundred telephone calls to find one person who would qualify to answer our survey, we would be dialing thousands of numbers before we could obtain a sample size that would be useful for our analyses.

The major disadvantage of this method is that some consumer groups are difficult to reach with online surveys. The elderly and consumers with very low incomes are notable examples of people who may not be online as much as other groups. If they are online, they may not be as comfortable taking a survey over a computer. Because these groups are small but important, it's essential when designing a study to be aware that one may be excluding a group whose opinions should be heard.

In-Person Surveys

The major advantage of using in-person surveys is that they catch people right after they have engaged in a behavior (e.g., purchased clothing), tried a product (e.g., drank a beverage), or had an experience (e.g., attended a seminar). Using traditional quantitative methods such as Internet or mail surveys allows time for memories to fade, which could lead to a biased recollection of the event and respondents' thoughts and feelings at the time. If you intercept people right after they have had an experience, you will be more likely to get the most accurate perception.

We have surveyed people in a variety of situations in order to understand their perceptions of stores, events, and particular products or services. One of my favorite studies was for a consumer-goods company that wanted to understand if an informational computer assisted shoppers when purchasing their products. The company created a personal shopping assistant that shoppers accessed on a personal computer in the middle of the store. The company created several prototypes and placed them in stores. We then intercepted customers after they were done shopping and asked them if they had used the assistant and what they thought about it. We were able to discern how many customers actually approached the computerized assistant, how likely they were to use it again, and if the assistant gave them good or poor shopping recommendations. These research results told the company that the current shopping assistant wasn't useful to customers and that it didn't provide good recommendations. The company decided to walk away from its invention as a result and saved millions of dollars.

We have also recruited people to facilities where they try products and then answer a survey about their perceptions of these products and their likelihood to purchase them. We regularly use this method to test our clients' products against competitor products, and the results have been very predictive of how well these products perform in the marketplace.

One disadvantage of this technique is that respondents generally can only give a few minutes of their time if you intercept them in their environments. Intercept surveys of ten minutes are long. The average interview is about three to five minutes, so the survey has to be thoughtfully crafted to make the most of this short time period. However, if you recruit individuals to a facility and have them try products, you can have a longer interview. Facility situations are somewhat less realistic but can be very useful for getting unbiased feedback about products and services.

Telephone Surveys

Telephone surveys used to be one of the most widely used methods and were once as popular as Internet surveys are today. One advantage of this technique is that almost everyone has a telephone, while some do not have Internet access. In addition, a live interviewer can determine if the respondent understands the question and can repeat it if necessary. A respondent can also ask questions and get clarification if a question is unclear. Furthermore, an interviewer might be able to dissuade a respondent from hanging up if he gets bored by the questions. She might sense that her respondent is getting bored and say, "Just a couple more minutes." The last advantage of telephone surveys is that you can program skip patterns into them. Thus, if a respondent has a particular belief, follow-up questions can explore that belief in detail.

One of the major disadvantages of telephone surveys is that people filter out calls from people they don't know. Caller ID services allow people to see whether a family member or friend is calling. If a caller is not someone they know, people may be less likely to answer the telephone. Another major disadvantage concerns cell-phone numbers. Approximately 13 percent of U.S. households do not have a traditional landline phone and only use a cell phone (Skeeter 2007). Cell-phone numbers are not listed in many traditional databases and Federal law prohibits the use of automated dialers when calling cell-phone numbers. The Pew Research Center estimates that it costs four to five times as much to interview respondents who only have a cell phone (Skeeter 2007). As a result, cell-phone-only respondents are often excluded from many studies. Cell-phone-only respondents, however, may differ from those who have traditional landline telephones in significant ways. They are more likely to be younger, more likely to be African American or Hispanic, less likely to be married, and less likely to be homeowners (Skeeter 2006).

Mail Surveys

Mail surveys provide an opportunity to contact people who are not easily reached through the Internet or by telephone. We used this method for a study we conducted with a group of residents of California who had immigrated to the United States and who spoke little or no English. Conducting a telephone survey would have been prohibitively expensive given all the different languages we were targeting and the small percentage of people who spoke each one. We decided to conduct a mail survey that was translated into twelve different languages. This approach was a successful way of reaching each of the groups that we were interested in surveying.

The major disadvantage of mail surveys is that it's difficult to have the level of question specificity that you can have with telephone or Internet surveys. You cannot program skip patterns into mail surveys, and respondents do not easily follow instructions to skip in and out of questions. It's not always easy for respondents to follow logic such as, "Skip to Q.23 and answer Section A." Mail surveys can also be expensive when you consider the cost of postage, particularly if the surveys are mailed to a large sample of people.

Mixed Methods

One way to overcome the disadvantages of any method is to use a mixed-method design. You can combine two or even three different methods. For example, in a recent piece of work, we wanted to survey low-income consumers who shop at discount stores. We learned that many of these customers lived in rural areas, and some didn't have Internet access. However, conducting mail or in-person intercept surveys with this group would have been very expensive. We suggested a mixed design that involved surveying customers who were online and then augmenting this data with surveys of customers who had been shopping in the stores and who were not online. Thus, we had the advantages of the Internet survey and its ability to drill into specific issues across a wide range of people. And we had the advantages of an in-person survey to talk with people who had just been shopping so we could get their immediate reactions to the stores. This method allowed us to talk to shoppers who were online and those who were not.

Emerging Methods

In addition to the major methods that I've discussed, there are many emerging qualitative and quantitative research tools that are being tested by market researchers. Some of these methods include Internet video diaries, where respondents record their thoughts and feelings via webcam for researchers to analyze. Another promising method involves using webcams in online discussion forums so moderators and participants can see one another. This method addresses some of my objections about not being able to read the body language of respondents in current online forums. Other methods that show promise use the cell phone. Respondents can answer a survey after trying a product or having an experience and thus provide real-time responses within their actual environment. Respondents can also be prompted by their phone to engage in certain behaviors (e.g., take medication) and then provide feedback at certain time intervals (e.g., report how they are feeling after a few hours). Researchers can also engage in interactive, qualitative research by using text messaging to ask questions and receive responses. Many of these new methods are still in their infancy, but they show great promise for the future.

4

Obtaining the Depth
Required for Insight

Once we identify the strategic question and design the study, the real work begins. It's not enough to assume that because we've done everything right up to this point, the answer will fall into our lap. Insight is the result of looking at something deeply and seeing it in a different way, which leads to that "aha." It's the level of depth that makes the difference. Over the years, I've noticed that there are several practices that can help in obtaining the depth required for real insight. If one is conducting qualitative research, there may be an opportunity to observe something no one has seen before or to ask a question in a way that yields a nugget of wisdom. There are also opportunities to manage a research project so that the process reveals a deeper understanding as the project continues.

Hearing beyond the Words

One thing that I've learned is that you have to interpret what people tell you to understand what they really mean. For example, some respondents don't want to tell you how they really feel about a product because they worry about hurting someone's feelings. Despite assurances that I have had nothing to do with the creation of a product, I distinctly get the feeling that some people are trying to be polite by not telling me that the product we're discussing is a real stinker. One of the things that respondents will say is that a service is great for someone other than themselves. When they tell me, "It would be great for my aunt or my mother, but not for me," I know that they would never purchase it. The other thing that people say is that they can't imagine using a certain product now, but they think they might use it in the future. The translation of that sentence is, "I don't like it or need it now, but I might change my mind." If they don't want it now, I have no reason to believe they will want it in the future.

I pay close attention to what people say about when they think they will purchase something. Respondents' estimates on timing often reveal the truth about their purchase intent. I recently did focus groups with wealthy consumers in which we tested a new type of luxury mattress. We first talked about the concept and then showed them the specific mattress. All the consumers loved it. I asked them if they would purchase this mattress and most said they would. I then told them to imagine that the mattress is currently available and asked how soon they would purchase it. Most of them said they would purchase it in a couple of years. The fact that respondents could not envision buying the mattress for a couple of years told me that they were not completely sold on it. When I probed them about the reason for their timing, many admitted that they had some doubts about this particular mattress.

Another thing that people sometimes say is to "make it cheaper" after they learn the price of a product. Consumers want to maximize their money, and they have a selfish interest in telling us to make products less expensive for them. However, something else is going on here. When respondents tell us that something should be less expensive, what they're really saying is that the product does not provide enough value for them. Unless the price is inflated, the issue is not the cost. Americans are willing to pay good money for all kinds of things. If something is perceived as providing a significant value to them and their loved ones, they will buy it. When people tell us to make something cheaper, they are generally telling us that whatever we're discussing is not something that provides enough benefits for them to buy it. If the issue really is price, we can discern this problem by asking what people would pay. On many occasions, we have seen that respondents will give a nominal figure in response, which tells us that a service has little value for them.

Sometimes it's not what people say, but what they do. We did a project for a personal-care company, and the client was interested in understanding how women select shampoo. We convened a focus group of women and asked them what was important for them when it came to shampoo. The women told us that a shampoo couldn't dry out their hair and that it had to leave their hair feeling soft and silky. They told us that a shampoo couldn't be too expensive, but if it made their hair look good, it was worth a few extra dollars. We then put out several bottles of shampoo on the table, and the women immediately opened the bottles and smelled the shampoo. Interestingly none of the women had mentioned fragrance as a major reason for buying shampoo, but it became obvious that fragrance was a major aspect of the purchase decision. Fragrance is probably the first thing women evaluate in a shampoo, followed by its performance. In so many different studies, it's the things that people don't say that speaks volumes. I discuss nonverbal communication in the next chapter and how you can read the hidden communication of research respondents.

Asking the Same Question in Different Ways

Generally, qualitative research projects involve creating a discussion guide and then following the general flow of the guide in a somewhat conversational form. Often the same question is asked of many different groups to determine if there is some consistency among people in their responses. However, one of the most useful techniques you can employ in qualitative research is to ask a question in numerous ways to understand the parameters of an answer. One of the frequently quoted examples of this phenomenon is about shaving. Typically, men complain about having to shave every day, and they regard the process as a bit of a nuisance. However, one clever moderator asked how men would feel about a product that would effectively make shaving a memory. Suddenly the men started to explain that shaving is an important masculine ritual and that losing that ritual would be undesirable. By asking about shaving in a variety of ways, the moderator learned the myriad thoughts and feelings men have about this subject.

There are many ways to ask the same question. The shaving example asks people to imagine their lives without something. Other techniques include asking respondents to imagine that they are the CEO of a specific brand and inquiring about what they would do differently. We've also asked people what a good advertisement would be for a new service. In some studies we've asked people to design the perfect product or service experience based on their current needs. All of these approaches reveal important things about what respondents really think and feel about something.

Probing and Probing

Another way to gain depth in qualitative work is to spend a great deal of time probing respondents' answers to questions. I generally do not take the first

27

response to my question as the final answer. It's usually more complicated than that. So when respondents tell me that they like something, I ask them what they specifically like about it, and then I ask which things they like most, and so on. I once had a client who told me that diabetic patients didn't mind having diabetes, and she sent me some focus group tapes to prove her point. The moderator had a group of diabetic respondents, and she asked them what it was like to have diabetes. Many of them responded that it was something that could be problematic but that they had gotten used to it. The moderator then went on to another question. As a result of her lack of probing, the client interpreted the first response as the final answer. If the moderator had probed about what was problematic about diabetes and what the respondents had specifically gotten used to, she would have understood the emotional response to this disease much better.

Managing a Qualitative Project to Achieve Depth

Another major way to achieve depth in qualitative research is to manage the project so that subsequent focus groups, interviews, or discussion forum sessions do not duplicate the previous ones. One of my mentors used to remind me that the word *focus* in "focus group" refers to getting a clearer, more focused understanding of the issues over time. He recommended having a different discussion during the last focus group session than during the first one. He believed that the initial superficial conversations change over time and become more thoughtful. By the time the groups are finished, the initial learning has been explored to a much deeper level.

This technique is called the reiterative approach, and we use it effectively for many different kinds of projects. We use this approach frequently with communications work. Our advertising agency partners will observe focus groups through a two-way mirror and then revise concept statements, taglines, and advertising communications between the groups based on what we've learned in each session. The result is that we have materials that are almost final by the end of several focus groups.

The other technique we use is to inquire what questions client observers have between sessions. Usually a set of questions will lead to more questions and so on. This reiterative question approach engages the observers of the research and shows the moderators what they need to focus on and explore more deeply. In a recent project that I did for a discount store, the client was adamant that she needed answers to particular questions. Once she had answers to these initial questions, new ones emerged. The answers to the new questions in turn begot more questions. This project is a good example of one for which the last focus group was completely different than the first one and for which we had a thorough understanding because we used this reiterative approach.

Testing Specific Hypotheses

Another way to obtain depth in both qualitative and quantitative research is to test specific hypotheses. Conducting strategic market research involves understanding what the hypotheses are in an organization and then testing them. In a project that we did for a large medical association, the client hypothesized that the physician members of this association would be likely to accept a new program if it didn't take up too much of their time and if it was beneficial for their patients. We described the new program to physicians by mentioning these qualities. We learned that the client was correct in her assertion that members would be likely to participate for the reasons she described. The problem was that the program was perceived as very time-consuming and ineffective in helping patients. We found instead that physicians were likely to participate if they were compensated.

Testing Potential Scenarios

One of my clients is a private equity firm that invests in other companies. They sometimes determine if they want to make an investment based on quantitative market research about an industry and a specific company within it. One way they evaluate a potential acquisition is by measuring how the customers of that company will respond to different scenarios. These scenarios could be actions that the future owners might take once they own the company, or they could be the actions of major competitors. In some cases we've tested what would happen if a major competitor offered a similar product or service or undercut the target investment company on pricing. These scenarios give my client a unique view of whether the company they are thinking of acquiring provides something that is uniquely valuable in the marketplace and how problematic it would be if competitors took certain actions.

You can test potential scenarios in both quantitative and qualitative research. In quantitative work, you can present specific scenarios and then measure consumers' likelihood to purchase. In qualitative work, you can test scenarios with questions such as: "What if a competitor offered you a similar product?" or "What if this service became more expensive?" or "What if a competitor offered the same service for less money?" We also ask respondents to imagine

29

brands offering new products and services: "What if Brand X now offered this potential product?" The qualitative and quantitative answers to these questions can yield invaluable information and tell us how loyal people are, how much people would be willing to pay for things, and how easily certain products can be replaced.

Another way to test scenarios quantitatively is with conjoint and discrete choice analysis. This type of analysis is just one major "what if?" question that is used to evaluate different product configurations. Respondents are offered several product configurations, such as: 1) a Chevrolet four-door sport-utility with eight cylinders for $39,999, or 2) a Toyota four-door sport-utility with six cylinders for $28,999. In this case, the brand, price, and number of cylinders are different and the number of doors is the same. Respondents are given many different car configurations and asked how likely they would be to purchase each one. These ratings allow us to determine how important different features are in specific products so we can simulate different offerings in the market and estimate demand for them. We have also done qualitative conjoint projects in the context of focus groups to understand the role that different features play in making a product or service more or less attractive.

Using Skip Patterns in Quantitative Research

Another way to gain depth in quantitative research is to use skip patterns in telephone and Internet surveys. These patterns will skip respondents in and out of questions without them knowing that the questions apply only to them. So the people who prefer Pepsi over Coke will be asked a set of questions about their perceptions of Pepsi, how often they buy it, when they buy it, and so on. Those who prefer Coke will be asked questions that specifically relate to Coca-Cola products. Those who do not have a preference will be asked about their perceptions of the two brands, how the brands are similar or different, how often the respondent drinks the products of each brand, and so on. Thus, we have really conducted three questionnaires in the context of one major survey. The result is that we can create a longer overall survey, but because it goes into depth for each segment, it is not too long for each respondent.

Using Open-Ended Questions in Quantitative Research

The last way we can obtain depth in quantitative research is by offering respondents the option to write in their thoughts and feelings in an open-ended format. We often ask people to explain what they like or dislike about a product and whether it has performed according to their expectations. Respondents may write a sentence or a paragraph about their experiences or perceptions of something. These responses are then evaluated by experts who group these responses into "codes." Codes are the common responses that people give to each question. Each response is assigned to one or more codes, and we calculate the percentage of people who volunteered that reason or perception. Thus, we might find that one of the things people like about a refrigerator is its color because 35 percent of people volunteered that response as a major reason they prefer the refrigerator they purchased.

Another way that we use open-ended responses is to allow respondents the chance to write in their own reason or perception if it is not represented in the response categories of a question. Survey designers often think they have exhausted all potential response categories when they write a question, but respondents may feel differently. Thus, we offer them the opportunity to write in their responses, usually in an "other" category. These open-ended answers are then coded, and the percentage of people who gave each response is tabulated. Occasionally you will find that one response surfaces among a large percentage of respondents. Other times, you may find that very little useful data emerges, which lets you know that you captured the most important response categories in the survey. Although open-ended questions can sometimes be expensive, they are well worth it.

5

Reading the Hidden Communications of Research Respondents

Sometimes it's what respondents *don't* say that can be the most revealing. In general, body language, or nonverbal communication, is a rich source of insight about what people think and feel about the topic one is researching. I like to say that you can choose not to speak, but you can never be silent nonverbally. I spend a great deal of time watching respondents' body language because they sometimes tell me more with their bodies than they do with their words. Regardless of whether you are a moderator or a person observing research respondents, being able to read body language can be very useful.

In this chapter, I discuss PERCEIVE, which is the method of reading nonverbal communication that I developed many years ago. It is one way of "perceiving" other people that I have found useful because it sums up all the parts of the complex system of nonverbal behavior. It's also easy to remember. Each letter of PERCEIVE refers to a major piece of nonverbal communication. "P" stands for proximity, "E" is for expressions, "R" is for relative orientation, "C" is for contact (physical touching), "E" is for eyes, "I" is for individual gestures, "V" is for voice, and the last "E" stands for existence of adaptors, which are those small fidgety behaviors that people do when they're stressed or bored.

You may be wondering how PERCEIVE was developed and what the basis is for it. Why not OBSERVE or SEE or ASPARAGUS? PERCEIVE was born after an exhaustive review of hundreds of studies that were conducted by academic researchers. The research literature revealed some basic findings about nonverbal communication that have been replicated in numerous studies. PERCEIVE is based on a summary of this body of research, and it describes the major areas of nonverbal communication: the face, body, voice, and hands. As an aside, this research was mostly conducted in English-speaking societies such as the United States, Canada, and Australia, and the findings accurately summarize Western cultures. The basic principles of what we will discuss, however, apply to most societies.

Proximity

Proximity refers to the amount of distance people place between themselves and others. Generally people tend to sit and stand near people they like and want to get to know. They tend to stand away from those whom they dislike or believe they have little in common with. I always find it interesting that people tend to sit and stand near those who are similar to them. I cannot tell you how many times all the women in a focus group have sat together and how often the men have done the same thing. This phenomenon also occurs with race. People of similar races tend to sit near one another. In a recent focus group I conducted in the Southern United States, all the African Americans sat on one side of the table, while all the Caucasians sat on the other side.

As a moderator I watch whom people sit and stand near. I also watch the degree of proximity that they have to me as a moderator. Not surprisingly, when people are engaged and interested in a topic, they tend to sit forward in their chairs and to lean toward the moderator; their proximity *increases*. When they are disinterested and disengaged, their proximity *decreases*. I also watch how closely respondents sit and stand next to one another in observational research, in-home interviews, and shop-along research. The closer the relationship, the closer the proximity tends to be between two people.

Expressions

Expressions refer to facial expressions that people make regularly. Researchers who study facial expressions across cultures have found that there are six basic emotional expressions that all cultures recognize and have a word to describe. These basic expressions are happiness, sadness, anger, fear, surprise, and disgust (Ekman & Friesen 1975). Some theorists believe that contempt is a basic expression, but others disagree. I will include it in our discussion. These basic expressions may be hardwired into us as a species, and all other expressions use some form of these basic ones (Ekman & Friesen, 1975). For example, you might have an expression that is partly surprise and partly happiness if you walk into your own surprise birthday party.

In general, people do not show exaggerated facial expressions. There are cultural display rules that dictate which emotional expressions are appropriate for specific situations. Thus, if your boss suggests that you stay late to work on a project, you probably wouldn't want to openly express anger to her. Although you're not thrilled, you will be professional and politely explain that you can stay for a couple of hours tonight and that you will come in early tomorrow to finish your work. Your expressions are in line with the cultural display rules for this situation. You didn't express anger—or did you?

Researchers have learned that when people feel something, they actually express something called a microexpression, which is an expression that lasts for about one-fifth of a second and is not typically seen by others (Ekman 2003). The reason this expression occurs is because we are hardwired to express certain emotions—particularly those basic ones just described. When we start to feel something internally, that feeling triggers muscles in our faces. We suppress a full expression before it occurs, and the result is a microexpression, which lasts for such a short period of time that a very small percentage of people will notice it. Have you ever seen a flash of an expression, but weren't sure if you saw something? You probably saw a microexpression.

Microexpressions are extremely useful in research situations because they reveal the immediate reactions that respondents have to products, services, brands, people, and specific parts of a discussion. The momentary expression yields valuable insight into what respondents are really feeling and thinking. As a moderator, when I see a microexpression, I don't call attention to it, but I allow the respondent to tell me another point of view. For example, in an in-home interview that we conducted with couples about financial services, a wife had a microexpression of contempt in response to some of the financial services her husband had purchased. After I saw the expression, I said that some people like these services and others do not. I asked her to tell me some of the reasons that people don't like these services. She could then tell me why she didn't like the financial services her husband bought without embarrassing him.

Seeing and reacting to microexpressions is not something that comes naturally to most people. One of the pioneers in this area is Paul Ekman. He created a CD-ROM that you can purchase to train yourself how to spot these expressions. After I trained myself to spot them, I was amazed at how often they occur. If the CD is not available, I encourage you to watch interviews in which the interviewer asks some controversial questions. If you slow down the recording, you can often see microexpressions on the faces of the people being interviewed.

Relative Orientation

Relative orientation refers to the degree of orientation that people have toward others. In general, the more interested we are in people, the more directly we orient ourselves toward them. Look at the next picture on the left. The couple in this picture is oriented almost directly toward one another. One of the first signs that an interaction between two people is beginning is that they start to orient their bodies toward one another. One of the first signs that an interaction is ending is when one or both people start to turn their bodies away. See the next picture on the right for an example. In this photo, the woman pictured on the right has started to turn her body away. Often you can tell who is interested in whom by a person's orientation. In a few focus groups I have had a respondent who wanted to be a moderator herself. She looked at the focus-group experience as a way to dominate a discussion. I could generally spot this situation within the first ten minutes of the group by her orientation. If she wanted to moderate the group, she would tend to orient herself toward the rest of the group members and away from me. I have a way of handling this situation that is very effective. I use my own orientation and other nonverbal cues to establish my authority.

Direct Orientation

Ending a Conversation

Orientation can tell us how engaged people are with others. In the situation described above, some of the respondents did not like the respondent's attempt to moderate the focus group, and they oriented themselves away from her and toward me. I always notice orientations when doing in-home interviews. Sometimes a couple is more oriented toward each another than they are toward the interviewer. Sometimes that's the way I like it. Sometimes in focus groups, the respondents are more focused on one another than on the moderator. It becomes a true group discussion that does not need a facilitator, and the orientations of the respondents show that fact. I like that also.

Contact

Contact refers to physical contact between two people. Physical contact is somewhat scripted among strangers and typically occurs with a handshake when people say hello or good-bye. However, outside of this scripted handshake, physical touch indicates liking, comfort, and familiarity with another person. Thus, we tend to touch those we like, those we are most familiar with, and those we are comfortable enough to touch.

Because touching is scripted among strangers, respondents generally do not touch me during interviews. However, respondents will occasionally shake my hand if they have been affected by their participation in a research project. Respondents will also touch one another if they have a close relationship or if they have been affected by another person. In some of my sessions, respondents become very emotional about an experience they are having. In a project with people who have a pulmonary disease, the respondents started to talk about how they cope with their situation. A young woman was not dealing well with her health, and the woman next to her encouraged her with several slight touches on the shoulder. Her touch of the other woman was an effort to comfort her, but it also revealed that she liked the young woman enough to touch her.

Respondents who know one another well sometimes touch each other and their physical contact, or lack thereof, can say a lot about their relationship. The closer and stronger the relationship, the more people tend to touch. I always notice if a couple touches each other during an in-home interview. I also notice how closely they sit together. My experience has been that couples who are in distress tend to sit the farthest apart and do not touch each other at all. In contrast, happier couples tend to sit closely and will occasionally touch each other.

Eyes

It has been said that the eyes are the window to the soul, and that statement may have more than a bit of truth to it. Our eyes reveal who we like and what captures our attention. We tend to look more frequently at the people and things we like and find interesting, and we also tend to look at them for a longer duration. One can tell when people are in love because they look at each another for long periods of time. People who do not like one another will rarely engage in eye contact unless they are being openly confrontational. Interestingly, we betray our prejudices with our eyes. In a classic study on racial prejudice, researchers learned that those who are prejudiced against African Americans look at them for a shorter period of time during interviews than individuals who are not prejudiced (Dovidio et al. 1997). The interesting thing about this finding is that people were unaware that they were looking at one group for less time than the other. Thus, our eyes say all kinds of things about who we like and who we don't like.

In market research, I notice how long people look at products and services that we show them. The longer folks tend to look at things, the more they tend to be interested in them. The less they look at things, the less they tend to like them. I also notice how long people look at one another in a group discussion.

People tend to look at those whom they like and respect. In almost every focus group, one person may have a strong point of view that he shares with the group. The duration that people look at him tells me how much they share his point of view and whether they like him.

Eye behavior can also tell you a great deal about who the leader is in a group or who has influence in a relationship. Sometimes people will look at their husband or wife when they answer a question to confirm that they are saying the correct thing. Sometimes people even look to me when I am moderating a focus group to determine if they've said the right thing. I discourage them from looking to me for any type of affirmation because there is no right or wrong answer in market research.

Eye behavior also tells us about how cognitively complex an issue is for someone to discuss. Generally when people access a memory or figure out an answer, they tend to look away. If I asked you right now to multiply two large numbers, you would probably look away to do the calculation and then come back to this page. The same is true for anything that we are figuring out or remembering. If I asked you to think of the names of several friends from third grade, you would probably look away to think about your memories from that time and the names of your friends. After you remember these names, you would then look back to this page. These eye behaviors are useful because the amount of time that people look away tells how close their answers are to the tops of their minds. If people have to look away to answer basic questions, such as where they grew up or what they do for a living, I begin to wonder if they are being entirely truthful.

Eyes Reveal Cognitive Complexity

The last thing that eye behavior reveals is whether something is emotionally difficult to discuss. People tend to look away when they are talking about something that they are ashamed of or that is embarrassing. They will also look away if something is difficult to discuss because it is emotionally evocative. Looking away allows people to gain control of their emotions, which is why people break eye contact. I watch eye behavior closely and notice if something seems difficult for a person to discuss. In those situations, I may redirect the conversation and come back to the topic later. I may also say that these things can be difficult to discuss as a way to reassure someone. By being sensitive to what a person is feeling about a conversation, we can learn more about her thoughts and feelings without making the situation uncomfortable for her.

Individual Gestures

Individual gestures are one of my favorite things to watch when respondents talk. There are two basic types of gestures: *emblems* and *illustrators*. Emblems are gestures that have a direct translation to a word or phrase. Most people within a culture will know the translation for these gestures. Examples of these emblems in American culture are the gestures for "OK," "Be quiet," "Shame on you," "He's crazy," and so on. These are common gestures that most people understand. See the next pictures for examples of emblems.

Emblem for 'Be Quiet'

Emblem for 'Good' or 'OK'

The other type of gesture is an illustrator, which does not have a clear verbal translation and seems somewhat random at first glance. However, it can convey a great deal of meaning. Illustrators often reveal an image in someone's mind and his perceptions of the world. Some of the things that these gestures can convey are:

- How things are grouped (e.g., brands, companies, types of products or services)
- How far apart things are (e.g., how closely aligned groups, people, ideas, brands, etc. are in someone's mind)
- Where things are located in a physical space (e.g. how far away something is, where something is located in reference to something else)
- The shapes of objects
- How large or small things or ideas are for a person
- How we use something (e.g., an appliance)
- The order of things or the steps that are taken to achieve an outcome
- To whom we are referring
- Ideas or beliefs that are important to us

Respondents gesture all the time, and they often tell me things that people don't even realize they're revealing. For example, companies often want to know how people group their products with those of competitors. When people are talking, they will often put similar brands in the same space. You can watch how closely they place them together to see which companies are perceived as most similar. Respondents will also gesture about how large or small they perceive a company or brand to be. They will also paint scenes in front of you with their hands, and if you look closely, you can see the images that they are visualizing in their minds. People will describe what things look like, how large they are, and what their shape is with their gestures. One of the best examples of this is to ask someone to give you directions and watch how she starts gesticulating about where you need to go. She is literally translating her view of your journey with her hands. The following photos show some examples of what gestures can convey.

Gesture Showing How Closely Two Brands are Aligned

Gesture Showing the Size of an Idea

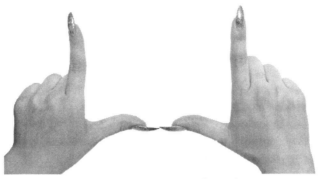

Gesture Showing Shape of a Product

Gestures also reveal how people use products. In some instances we realized that respondents were dissatisfied with a product because they were using it incorrectly. Their gestures showed us how they used an appliance, and it became clear that some of them had not read the directions and were having problems. Respondents will also indicate the order in which they do things with gestures. They will lay out the first step, the second one, and so on. When people explain these things to us, we get a better understanding about all the things they need to do for certain activities like making certain types of foods or planning a vacation. What may seem so straightforward may not be so when you see all the steps that are necessary.

Respondents also reveal the people they are thinking about or the beliefs they hold most deeply through gestures. They reveal these things through subtle (and not so subtle) pointing. On more than one occasion, people will give an example and will subtly point to a person they believe represents that example. They don't think they're overtly pointing to anyone, and they don't even realize that they're betraying their view of that person. On some occasions, the person being referred to doesn't realize it, either, but in other cases, it's more obvious. The other thing that respondents do is to motion toward themselves or point to their chest when talking about something that is very important to them or that is a deeply held conviction. I remember watching a politician on television who pointed to his heart as he explained to the crowd, "This is something that we strongly believe." His gesture revealed that the issue was something in which *he* strongly believed. That same politician then pointed to the audience and said: "This is something that we need to do." His gestures said that it was something that he wanted the audience to do.

Respondents also tend to gesture more when they are confident or enthusiastic about something. If you watch people speak you can see that the largest gestures tend to occur around the words or phrases that they are emphasizing in their speech. I always find it interesting to see what topics lead to gesturing. I once ran a workshop with businesspeople about reading nonverbal communication. I had the participants do an exercise in which they talked about various things and observed their partner's gestures. One man didn't have a partner, so I went over to do the exercise with him. He promptly told me that he never gestures, and he didn't—until we started talking about a topic that wasn't a part of the exercise. We started talking about his kids, and he started gesturing. Obviously, this was a topic about which he was very enthusiastic. People differ in the amount that they gesture, but most people will gesture a little bit when talking about something that is important to them.

Voice

The voice reveals many things. One thing it reveals is our emotions. People betray their emotions with the pitch, volume, and speed of their speech. For example, people tend to speak more slowly when they're sad and they tend to use lower pitches. When people are happy, they tend to speak more quickly. Interestingly, people tend to use higher pitches when they're stressed. We are surprisingly able to read the emotions of speakers even if we cannot see them. The emotional states that we're most able to recognize are anger, happiness, boredom, interest, contempt, and sadness. Disgust and shame are harder to decode (Pittam & Scherer 1993; Banse & Scherer 1996).

Reading voices becomes important particularly when one is conducting in-depth telephone interviews. We know from researchers that one can tell another person's age, gender, and social class just from listening to her voice (Remland 2000). The voice can also reveal whether someone is an extrovert or an introvert. Extroverts tend to talk quickly, moderately loudly, and fluently, and tend to have longer utterances. Introverts, in contrast, tend to talk slowly, somewhat quietly, less fluently, and they speak in shorter utterances.

The voice also reveals when something is difficult to discuss or when it is cognitively complex. People tend to pause when they are either accessing a memory of figuring out an answer. The pause does the same thing that the eyes do when we look away to think about or remember something. People pause when trying to remember something that is not at the top of their minds. The other time that people pause is when they are having difficulty talking about something that is emotionally evocative for them. You can tell whether an issue is cognitively complex or difficult to discuss from observing the voice along with all of the other nonverbal behaviors.

Existence of Adaptors

Adaptors are those small, fidgety behaviors such as twirling a pen, rotating a ring, twisting one's hair, biting one's lip, or biting one's nails. People tend to have adaptors when they feel stressed or bored. Apparently adaptors help us deal with our boredom or stress because they give us an outlet for our feelings and pent-up energy. The interesting thing about these behaviors is that we share them with other primates. When a higher-status primate walks into a lower-status primate's environment, the lower-status one starts to show adaptors (Maestripier et al. 1992). He may play with his fur or pick at a stick, and he looks surprisingly human when he does this.

Examples of Adaptors Among Primates and Humans

Adaptors are useful things to watch because they reveal periods of stress or boredom. I watch for doodling in my focus groups because I know that if the conversation becomes relatively disinteresting that the number of adaptors in the room will increase. In some cases this situation cannot be helped. However, it does let me know that people may not be listening intently to the discussion. The existence of adaptors also tells me that someone may be stressed about a topic. In some interviews I've had with respondents about financial services, they have started to show adaptors when they talk about the financial decisions they have made for their families. The fact that people were showing adaptors may have revealed that they were uncomfortable with some of the decisions they made.

Years ago we did a study for a company about its Web site. We asked respondents to go onto two firms' Web sites (the company's Web site and a competitor's Web site) and do certain activities. We videotaped them while they were surfing and counted the number of adaptors that occurred while they were on each Web site. We then asked them to evaluate how user-friendly the Web sites were after they were finished. One Web site was much easier to navigate than the other. Respondents had many more adaptors when they were on the Web site that was difficult to navigate and very few adaptors on the easier Web site. We deduced the ease or difficulty of the Web sites just by counting the number of adaptors, and we were correct.

Putting it All Together

When I observe respondents in different research situations (e.g., in a home, in a store, in a focus-group facility), I observe all aspects of their nonverbal communication in addition to listening to what they have to say. Because everyone is different, there are some rules that I use when watching people. These rules are:

- Watch an individual for variations from his baseline
- Watch for variations from the normal situation
- Watch for variations expressed toward different people

Everyone is different, and some people are naturally more expressive than others. Thus, there is a baseline for every person. I watch variations from that baseline. If Kelsey is naturally expressive and she tells me nonverbally that she loves the new model of car I've shown her, I take her natural expressivity into consideration. Her verbal and nonverbal behavior say that she's pretty enthusiastic about a lot of things, and that she's an extroverted woman. However, if Michael is not particularly expressive and he becomes expressive after viewing an advertisement, his expressive behavior says something significant about the way the ad affected him. I also watch for variations from a particular norm. Certain situations call for a different level of expressivity, and groups create their own norms. If a focus group gets somewhat boisterous and high-spirited because it's occurring on a Friday afternoon, I watch for variations from that norm. Last, I watch for variations expressed toward different people. If Doug has one reaction to Bill Gates and another reaction to Bill Clinton, that provides me with important information about his feelings about each of these people.

Through observing all the different aspects of PERCEIVE, I watch for emotional reactions; ease or difficulty in talking about things; how complex issues are for people; how much people like or dislike one another; and how much they like or dislike the brands, products, and services that we show them. I also watch for deception and for behavior that tells me that the respondent is telling me what she thinks I want to hear. Sadly, the proliferation of the market research industry has created a group of people who are professional research respondents. These people make a significant amount of money going from study to study—a practice that I abhor. The nonverbal indicators of deception are very useful to me in ferreting out these folks.

6

Getting to the Heart of Respondents' Emotions

Emotions play a large role in how people view brands, products, and services. They also play a large role in purchase decisions for all groups of people. I've learned this fact from countless projects and by talking with so many different people over the years. Although people often give very rational reasons for their behavior, emotions are an important part of how they process information and how they make major and minor decisions. Good researchers realize that emotions can have a huge influence on people, regardless of whether it's physicians talking about the medications they prescribe or housewives talking about the makeup they purchase.

In our culture there is a common belief that good decisions occur when we subtract our emotions from the decision process and rely solely on reason. In actuality, the reverse is true. We tend to make better decisions when our emotions are involved, and we make worse decisions when they're not. Some of the most fascinating research in this area has been done with people who have normal cognitive functioning but cannot process emotional signals because of brain lesions. These people are the epitome of rational decision makers because they do not process any emotional information when deciding what to do. Contrary to popular thought, researchers have found that these unemotional decision makers actually make worse decisions (Bechara 2004). Apparently, making decisions based on gut feelings may not be such a bad idea after all.

So how do good researchers unearth the messy, sticky emotional world of the individuals they interact with for only a short period of time? We do it carefully. Respondents do not typically want to have a therapy session and delve into their inner emotional lives while participating in a research study. They do not want to resolve inner conflicts or understand how childhood experiences have marred them. However, we need to know the role that emotions play in a particular set of perceptions and behaviors. Getting to the heart of respondents' emotions involves using tools and techniques that allow participants to express their feelings in a way that makes them feel safe and that provides us with useful information. Some of the ways we obtain the emotional piece of a decision include:

- •Projection techniques
  - ◦ Projecting feelings onto other people
  - ◦ Projecting feelings onto characters
- •Associations
  - ◦ Word associations
  - ◦ Image associations
- •Accessing hopes, dreams, and aspirations
- •Storytelling
- •Salient memories

Creating the Right Atmosphere

Creating an atmosphere where emotional expression is acceptable and even encouraged is a key component to having respondents express themselves. Good moderators begin their sessions by encouraging people to be honest and to openly express their thoughts and feelings. They also use their nonverbal expressions to create a comfortable, accepting environment. When respondents express themselves openly and honestly, the moderator can respond nonverbally in ways that say that such sharing is acceptable, such as giving good eye contact and nodding when someone shares. As a result, people will begin to be expressive in response to one another, which can encourage more sharing of inner feelings. It is not unusual in some of my focus groups for the respondents to begin sharing things that are deeply personal and highly emotional, such as fears about a loved one dying, and then to have others expound on these emotional experiences in great depth. I've seen more than my share of tears from respondents who have felt comfortable enough to express their deepest feelings in a group discussion.

Projection Techniques

Another way to elicit respondents' emotions is to use projection techniques that allow people to share their feelings in a nonthreatening way. The common ones that we use are to ask respondents to imagine that someone else is experiencing something and to ask them how that other person feels. For example, we might be interested in all the fears that people have when buying a car, so we would ask them to describe feelings that other people have when they buy a car. We can specifically ask them to discuss any fears that people have during this process. This technique allows people to discuss their feelings without personalizing them. Projective exercises like this one are particularly useful with people who are uncomfortable describing some of their feelings because they do not want to appear vulnerable.

Another projective technique that we use involves characters. We use characters that represent thoughts and feelings and have respondents identify the character that is most like them. In one study we did with physicians, we put pictures of different characters up on the walls. Some of these characters were superheroes like Captain America, and some of them were Peanuts characters. In one picture, Snoopy was hanging on to a trapeze, but just barely. We asked the physicians to describe which character represented them, and several identified the scared Snoopy as the character that represented their reaction to treating certain diseases. The characters allowed them to express certain emotions in a way that was not threatening to them. However, in more formal focus group discussions, physicians tend not to divulge their feelings of fear and worry. We also use celebrities as a way to allow people to project their feelings onto others. Some celebrities, depending on the current tabloid news, can represent a variety of thoughts and feelings for people.

Associations

We also use the technique of associations to elicit emotional content. Sometimes we give the name of a brand and have people tell us the words they associate with it. Let's imagine that we're researching a brand of fictional toothpaste called "Natural Toothpaste." We would say the brand name, and then respondents would say the words they associate with this brand. After doing numerous interviews or focus groups, we might learn that specific words are strongly associated with this brand. For example, we might have learned that "snobby," "expensive," "rich," and "arrogant" are the words most associated with this brand. These words speak volumes about the emotions that people have about this brand. We could create a map that shows the

51

words that have the strongest associations with a particular brand (mentioned by the largest number of people) and the words that have associations that are somewhat weaker (mentioned by fewer people, but nonetheless mentioned). See Figure 1 for an example of this map.

Figure 1: Brand Map for Toothpaste

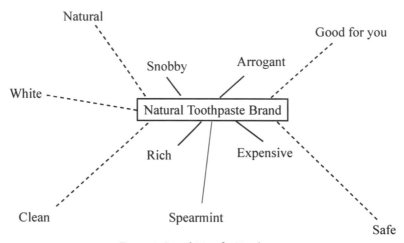

Figure 1: Brand Map for Toothpaste

Another effective technique for ascertaining some of the gut-level associations people have is to understand the imagery associated with a product or service. One way to do this is by having respondents create collages. We have stacks of popular magazines that we provide to respondents, and we ask them to cut out any image that reminds them of a brand. This technique is associative, so respondents tend to pull images that capture a thought or feeling they have about a product. Images constitute a different language for people because images convey a richer set of feelings than just words. In the end, we learn what the emotional underpinnings for something are. For example, a pharmaceutical company asked me to understand how a particular new medication is perceived by looking at all imagistic associations people have with this medication. We learned that people associate very specific colors and images with this medication. The result of this work was used to create the look and feel of this new brand. To see a fictional example of a beverage brand with certain imagery, see the next picture. As you can see in this hypothetical example, this brand has strong associations with movement, speed, physical activity, the outdoors, and sports.

Imagery Associated with Hypothetical New Beverage

Hopes, Dreams, and Aspirations

A very useful technique that we use is to engage people's hopes, dreams, and aspirations. By understanding a person's hopes and dreams, we can understand some of the emotions that he has about the things that he buys. I believe that people don't buy stuff; they buy visions of the future and perceptions of who they want to be. When a man buys exercise equipment, what exactly is he buying? I would argue that, at some level, he is buying a desired vision of himself, and that he sees a future person who looks good and who accrues certain rewards as a result. Clearly his hopes and dreams play a large role in his purchase decision. In numerous categories, we have discovered that people buy products and services to bolster a specific self-perception. We are always intrigued by people who are not wealthy, but who use everyday purchases like coffee to give themselves a feeling of luxury and show the world that they have money. In so many categories, a purchase is not just a statement about oneself, but a ticket to a lifestyle that people want. By understanding these desires, we are touching their emotional experience for that purchase. When people buy a time-share, are they buying a vacation, or are they hoping for more quality time with loved ones and better relationships with family members? The emotional piece of this decision is probably much stronger than other parts of it. When you understand the emotions, you've come a long way to understanding the decision to buy.

Stories and Memories

Stories are another way to understand the emotions that people have about products and services. We have people tell us stories about how they decided to purchase something and how they experience it. These stories may sound random at first, but when we start to look at stories across many people, we see common themes. We learned when we talked with young couples about their furniture purchases that these couples were not just telling us about the furniture in their homes, but they were often telling us the stories of their relationships. The purchase of furniture was often a symbolic behavior that meant commitment, permanency, and the blending of two styles into one. Thus, the emotions around furniture purchasing were very deep and quite central to the young couples in their quest for a new life together.

Memories are another way to understand the emotional part of decision making. We ask respondents to tell us salient memories they have of the times they have used products. We may ask them: "Tell us about the first time you heard of Pepsi," "What is your first memory of Pepsi?" "Which celebrities can you remember drinking Pepsi?" "Tell me about times with your friends when you were drinking Pepsi," and so on. All of these memories have an emotional valence to them, and they begin to sum up a person's experience of a brand. We look at these memories and analyze them because the emotional themes that run through these memories are similar across groups of people and reveal the emotional components of a brand.

7

Analyzing Numeric Data to Determine What Drives Markets

The way that data is analyzed can make the difference between a project that just provides information and a study that offers real insight. Our approach to data analysis is to start with our hypotheses and to test these ideas rather than to expect data to magically tell us a story. There are two schools of thought in the market research world. One school advocates doing a variety of analyses that are not driven by any underlying hypotheses as a way to mine the data and to see what pops up. The other school advocates a hypothesis-driven approach, in which you test your hypotheses about a market and learn what really drives it. I clearly subscribe to the school of thought that tests hypotheses, and I'll show you why this approach often works much better than just expecting the data to magically provide an answer.

Hypothesis-Driven Analyses

As already described in a previous chapter, we begin a project by understanding a client's hypotheses about their customers and markets. If clients cannot articulate any specific hypotheses, we help them to identify these ideas. Let's imagine that we're doing a project for a new type of television. We have the following hypotheses:

- •Gender hypothesis: men will be more likely than women to purchase this new TV

- •Age hypothesis: younger consumers will be more likely than older consumers to purchase this new TV

- •Income hypothesis: higher-income consumers will be more likely to purchase this new TV than will lower-income consumers

There are likely to be quite a few hypotheses that an organization generates. These hypotheses will in turn lead to more hypotheses. If these were the only three hypotheses that were identified, one resulting hypothesis is that young, high-income men would be the group most likely to purchase this TV. The group that would be the least likely to buy is hypothesized to be older, low-income women.

We then create a set of cross-tabulations that specifically tests these assertions. We divide the data by all three of these categories. We can look at the data for each group and determine if our hypotheses are supported or not. The best way to analyze these results is to conduct *t*-tests comparing each group's results. Thus, we can compare whether men are significantly more likely than women to purchase this TV, whether low-income people are less likely to purchase than high-income people, and so forth. This approach tends to lead to other hypotheses, which in turn lead to other analyses. So if we find that men are more likely to purchase this TV, we may hypothesize that they like the fact that it is new technology. We may do further cross-tabulations to look at people who appreciate that this TV is cutting-edge technology, so we can determine if these things are related to gender. The result is that we have a clear set of analyses that are directed by the early thinking we did when we commenced this project. These analyses allow us to eventually tell a story about the findings.

So what's wrong with the approach that lets the data speak for itself? The problem with just letting the data speak for itself is that it doesn't. Data doesn't magically appear with interesting results. We need to divide it and subdivide it and ask questions of it in order to fully understand a market. On many occasions people set up cross-tabulations without any sense of why one group might differ from another and without underlying explanations of why these differences would exist. Early in my career, I worked at a company with a man who loved statistics and who liked to throw all the variables from a study into different analyses because he assumed that that something interesting would appear. He would do correlations and cluster analyses with tons of variables, hoping to find some magical answer. The result was often reams and reams of paper with tons of numbers and no clear story about what the data said. He ended up becoming very frustrated and often could not provide great value to his clients.

Analyses to Determine What Predicts Perceptions and Behavior

Sometimes clients want to know what predicts purchasing behavior or what determines certain perceptions. The only way to accurately identify if something has an effect is to use an *experimental design*. An experimental design takes an *independent variable* and manipulates it in some way and then measures the effect of this manipulation on a *dependent variable*. When the only thing that changes is the independent variable, any effect on a dependent variable is due to that independent variable. Thus, you can measure the effect of color on the attractiveness of a specific car by manipulating only the color of a car and measuring perceptions of the attractiveness to see if color has an effect. You might learn that color has a large effect on perceptions of a VW Bug and that the car is much more attractive when it is shown in unusual colors.

We used an experimental design for a study that we conducted for the American Academy of Cosmetic Dentistry. They wanted to learn whether one's smile influences perceptions of attractiveness and personality. To determine whether a smile influences perceptions, we took pictures of eight individuals (four women and four men) and varied the smile. We used Photoshop so that the picture of the person was exactly the same—same clothing, same hair, and same facial expression. The only thing that was different was the smile. Each person was pictured two times. In one picture the person had white, straight teeth (the beautiful smile condition); in the other picture, the teeth were less white and not as straight (the regular smile condition). See the next picture for an example. We used a complicated research design in which everyone saw pictures of people that either had a beautiful smile or a regular smile. However, no respondent saw the same person with both smiles.

"Regular Smile" shown on left and "Beautiful Smile" shown on right

Respondents rated the pictured individuals on their attractiveness, intelligence, happiness, and career success, and on how friendly, interesting, kind, wealthy, popular with the opposite sex, and sensitive to other people they were. We then analyzed the data to determine if the type of smile made a difference when people had the beautiful smile instead of the regular smile. Because the only thing that varied was the smile, any differences in perceptions were because of the smile. We were amazed to learn that when people have a beautiful smile with white and straight teeth that people perceive them as more attractive, intelligent, happy, successful in their career, friendly, interesting, kind, wealthy, popular with the opposite sex, and sensitive to other people than when they do not have such a smile (Beall 2007). This study is an excellent example of how one can use an experimental design to determine what predicts specific perceptions.

In cases when one cannot do an experiment, you can learn which variables are related by using a correlation analysis. You can determine if gender, age, or income are highly correlated with purchasing a new TV by correlating these variables with actual purchases or respondents' stated intention to purchase the TV. Low correlations indicate that two things are not related to one another and that one variable does not vary with the other. High correlations indicate the opposite. Thus, we might find a high correlation between income and propensity to purchase a new TV. As income increases, the likelihood of purchasing this TV also increases. However, correlations do not indicate causation. Just because two things are highly correlated does not mean that one causes the other. Having a high income does not cause one to be interested in purchasing a new TV; it's more complicated than that.

Analyses to Determine the Major Segments in a Market

Another major question that organizations want to answer is what the major segments are in a market. They want to understand which specific groups are most likely to purchase their product and why. Organizations want to learn how large these groups are, what they are like demographically, and how to communicate effectively with them. By identifying the segments in the market, organizations can determine which groups they want to expend resources on and which ones will be most likely to respond. Segmentations are a way of describing a market as well as a way of providing direction for an organization's marketing efforts.

I am a strong advocate of segmentations that are customized for a specific company's product or service. I believe that unless a segmentation is based on data that is collected for that specific category, it will not be very useful. We have never seen a segmentation that is valuable for driving major strategic decisions in a business that was not created exclusively for that organization. We have seen numerous examples of marketing executives buying segmentations that can be purchased by anyone, including their competitors, and that ultimately provide little or no value. So if you want to know about the segments in the dog food market, conduct a segmentation study specifically about dog food and the major brands that play there. Don't buy a secondary segmentation that was designed for all businesses and expect to figure out the segments of dog-food buyers.

Our approach to segmentation is first to define which variable or variables are most critical for the organization. We determine this variable based on how the organization will use the segmentation. If the company is trying to predict which groups prefer specific brands, then the critical variable in the survey is which brand each respondent has bought or intends to buy. If the company wants to separate those who spend a lot from those who do not, then the critical variable is the amount of a product that purchasers buy. In many cases, the critical variable is purchasing that specific brand. Once we determine the critical variable, we will identify which variables are most closely associated with it and how they are related. After identifying the variables that are highly related with the critical variable, we will usually do a cluster analysis on these variables, or we will combine them in certain ways to create segments.

For example, let's say we're interested in cell phone usage and that we want to create a segmentation for a cell phone company (Carrier A). Let's imagine that our client cares most about identifying people who use a lot of cellular service and who are most likely to purchase their brand of service. They want to offer certain packages to these individuals. We might do an analysis that determines that age is highly related to cell phone usage and that younger consumers use cell phone service the most. We might determine that what predicts brand usage among young users is the cell phone service their parents are using. What might predict that brand usage among slightly older users is the brand their friends are using. We might end up with a segmentation that looks like this:

- **Segment 1**: Under-twenty-five-year-olds whose parents use Carrier A
- **Segment 2**: Under-twenty-five-year-olds whose parents use other carriers
- **Segment 3**: Thirty- to forty-year-olds whose friends use Carrier A
- **Segment 4**: Thirty- to forty-year-olds whose friends use other carriers
- **Segment 5**: Forty- to fifty-year-olds
- **Segment 6**: Fifty-one- to sixty-four-year-olds
- **Segment 7**: Sixty-five-plus-year-olds

We could then profile these groups to determine if their behavior and attitudes are what we predicted. Let's assume that our predictions are borne out in the data and that Segment 1 has the highest usage and the greatest loyalty toward Carrier A, followed by Segment 3. Thus the highest-priority segment would be Segment 1, followed by Segment 3. In this case, the company has clear direction on which segments are most valuable to them and which ones they should target first. Additional profiling of these groups in terms of their attitudes, usage, and desired services will allow the company to be able to offer services that these segments want and to communicate with them in ways that are productive.

Thinking about how a segmentation will be used down the road is a critical part of the analysis process. Many years ago, I worked for a consulting firm that used to do segmentations for Regional Bell Operating Companies (RBOCs, or local phone companies like Atlantic Bell, Ameritech, and Pacific Bell) who wanted to enter the long-distance market. Deregulation was in its infancy, and there were special rules about data usage. The local phone companies were not allowed to use their own data to target customers for long-distance service. Thus, any segmentation that we did for these companies had to use data that could be purchased from external data vendors. You may be asking why we were constrained in this way. The reason is because these companies intended to purchase large databases of information for a given geographic area and then to assign every household in the database to a segment. We created an algorithm that could be used to assign everyone to a specific segment. After assigning all households in a geographic area to segments, the company intended to contact people in specific segments with an offer to purchase long distance service from them. Thus, when we created the segments, we had to stick to variables that could be bought from the large data vendors. Thus, thinking through how the segments would be used and what the data constraints were for these companies was extremely important.

Sometimes a segmentation needs to serve different purposes for two different groups in an organization. We did such a segmentation for an educational foundation. We learned that there were two different ways of viewing this organization's customers. One part of the organization viewed customers in terms of the type of organizations that bought the foundation's educational materials. The other part of the organization viewed the customers in terms of how much they spent. Thus, we needed to create a segmentation that would address the needs of both of these client groups. We achieved this objective by identifying segments that overlapped. The eventual solution allowed the client to look at the segments as either organizational segments or as value segments. As you can see in Figure 2, the segmentation looks somewhat like a Rubik's Cube, and you can look at the segments in different ways. By addressing how the segmentation would be used by two groups down the road, we created a solution that is still used today.

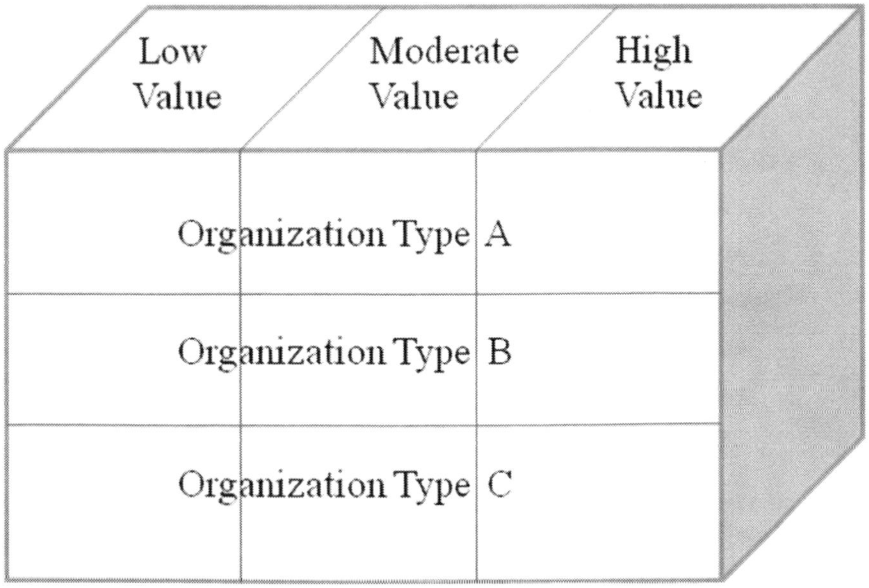

Figure 2: Segmentation that Views the Market in Two Different Ways

Analyses to Determine the Best Configuration for a Product or Service

Organizations often want to identify what the best configuration is for their product or service. For example, car manufacturers want to know what kinds of features to put on a luxury car that will create the greatest demand for it. They also want to know which features are most valued, so they can create the car that people are willing to pay a great deal to own. So how do you do that? We use conjoint or discriminant analysis to identify the best product configuration for certain groups of people or for a market overall. Conjoint or discriminant analyses are slightly different, but they offer the same thing to researchers. (Discriminant analysis enables you to control some configurations, whereas conjoint analysis does not.) They enable us to figure out what the potential demand is for a large number of product configurations. Let's imagine that we're trying to design an alarm clock. We first define the product attributes and then the levels of these attributes. We might come up with the following:

- •LCD display (attribute)
    - ◦ Large (level 1)
    - ◦ Small (level 2)
- •Alarm is:
    - ◦ Music
    - ◦ Music or loud sound
    - ◦ Music or loud sound or a bright light
- •CD Player
    - ◦ Present
    - ◦ Not present
- •Price
    - ◦ $35
    - ◦ $30
    - ◦ $25

We then show different configurations of alarm clocks to respondents and asked them how likely they would be to purchase each one. The number of alarm clocks and the particular configurations are determined by a model that we eventually use after the data is collected to simulate many configurations, including ones that we have not have tested. The result is a simulator in which you can see customer demand for any type of alarm clock that uses the attributes and levels that you tested. An example of a simulator is shown in Table 2.

	Alarm Clock 1	**Alarm Clock 2**	**Alarm Clock 3**
LCD Display	Large	Small	Large
Alarm	Music	Music or sound	Music, sound, or light
CD Player	Not present	Not present	Present
Price	$30	$25	$35
Etc	Etc	Etc	Etc
Market Size	100,000 people	100,000 people	100,000 people
Market Share	15%	20%	10%
Revenue	$450,000	$500,000	$350,000

Table 2: Example of Simulator Output

Optimizing products and services is an important part of product development. Organizations can use these simulators to see which configuration would compete best with the products that are currently available. They can also simulate potential competitor products to see how well their particular product configuration would compete with them. These tools are invaluable because they have so many different applications. You could use this tool to optimize the layout of your lunch room. We know of a case in which a large nonprofit organization considered using discriminant analysis to identify the best positioning and supporting statements for a national advertising campaign.

Other Analyses

There are a variety of statistical analyses that can be used to learn about markets for an organization. Table 3 shows some examples of the major questions that you can answer and the suggested statistical tools.

Example Question	Suggested Statistical Tool
How related are two variables? (e.g., how related are gender and income?)	Correlation
Which set of things is most related to a variable? (e.g., how are age, gender, and education related to income?)	Regression analysis
Are there significant differences between groups?	*t*-test, analysis of variance (ANOVA, F-test)
Do specific groups differ in a set of attitudes or group of behaviors?	Multivariate analysis of variance (MANOVA)
Are preferences for products or services similar or different than what would be expected by chance?	Chi-squared analysis
What is the underlying structure of a set of attitudes?	Factor analysis
What are the natural groups in a market?	Cluster analysis
What is the optimal configuration for a product or service?	Conjoint or discriminant analysis

Table 3: Example Questions and Suggested Statistical Tools

8

Interpreting Results
and Going beyond the Data

Often market researchers assume that the data is the answer. Approximately 53 percent of people prefer this product, so that's the one that should be launched, right? Well, it might seem like the right product, but it might not be the best one for that company. So if you can't just go by the data, how do you interpret results in a way that is useful? One of the best examples of this situation occurred early in my career when I was working with a brilliant consultant who ended up becoming a top executive at an ad agency in New York. We worked together on research for an online travel agency. He asked consumers what kind of name they would like for this travel agency, and the consumers tended to give pedestrian names like TravelAgency.com, BookTravel.com, and others. He then floated some names in front of these folks to get their reactions. Names that were fairly straightforward and somewhat boring tended to be liked the most. However, one name that was somewhat different and offbeat generated a mixed reaction. Some consumers liked it, and others hated it. The consultant recommended that the online company go with that name because it evoked a response. He wanted a name that would get a reaction—whether positive or negative. The online travel agency went with the offbeat name, and it's one of the most memorable names in that industry. That name is Orbitz.

Interpreting research results is not just about selecting the concept with the highest score or with the greatest percentage of respondents who like it. It's about looking deeper into the research and asking several questions. What are respondents really saying when they give something a high score? Does that mean that's the one they understood better than the others, or is that the one that they found the most believable? What are respondents really reacting to when they give us their feedback? Do they like the catchphrases and the graphics, or are they responding to some overarching idea that grabs them? By looking a little deeper at what people are telling us, we can begin to understand what is really occurring. In the Orbitz example, respondents were saying that they liked names that fit with the service. They wanted a name that they could understand. The travel company's ad agency, however, wanted a name that communicated new and different and that was memorable. Thus, when they evaluated consumers' responses to the names, they listened to the strength of the reactions to the names rather than whether consumers liked them because they were easy to understand.

When doing research, it's important to keep in mind that the evaluation criteria that consumers use may be different from the ones we use to help an organization. We recently did research for a large consumer-goods company that was selecting an ad agency. It decided to put the materials of two agencies up against each other to see which agency was better. Let's call these Agencies A and B. The consumers claimed that they liked Agency A's materials better than B's. The reason they liked A's materials was because they were colorful and pleasant to view. Agency B's materials were not as colorful or as attractive. However, when we dug more deeply into their responses to the materials, consumers told us that Agency B had a more innovative idea and that it was very alluring to them, but the materials turned them off. This consumer-goods company realized that having a big idea was the major differentiator between ads, and they eventually selected Agency B. It turned out to be an excellent decision for them.

As a general rule, we should not look to respondents to make business decisions. We don't just take whatever consumers prefer and recommend that as the answer. Interpreting market research in this way is naïve. We look at the reasons that something is preferred and make recommendations that make sense for the organization. When testing new products and services, we consider:

- How well does this product/service fit with this brand?
- How well could this company execute this product/service?
- Does this new product or service require a high level of advertising support to be successful?

On so many occasions, we have identified a winning product, but the company could not execute it well or did not provide the level of advertising it required. One of my favorite clients is a company that puts very little money into national advertising, and its innovative products never get the exposure they deserve. People typically will not buy new, innovative products unless they are aware of them and have been educated about their benefits. Sadly, this company doesn't do either of these things well. The result is that the innovative products it has created never sell as well as they should, given our research results.

Reporting Results and Telling a Story

After the data from a study has been collected, some market researchers take the discussion guide or a survey and then parrot back each finding for each section of the study. The result is a compendium of information and little direction on how to interpret it or what to do as a result. The information is then put on a shelf somewhere and pulled out when someone asks about that particular study. I've seen these books in some of my clients' offices, and I marvel at the wasted time, money, and paper. What is the point of gathering information just for the sake of having it? Information isn't useful unless it can be used to make major decisions.

When I first began my career in this field, my mentor asked me to put the words "So what?" on the wall in front of my desk. He instructed me to look at those words every time I looked at data and then to integrate that thinking into my reports. I remember being irritated with him because it seemed like the information should be enough, but it wasn't. Because I was trained in a consulting firm, we were coached to look at data as a means to help a business rather than mere information. I still look at research results that way. When I design questionnaires or conduct focus groups, I instinctively ask my clients: "If you knew that information, what would you do with that knowledge?" Knowing something is great, but only if you can act on the information. There is very little point to asking a question if the information cannot be used.

Because we take a strategic approach to market research, reporting of results follows all the work that we've done since the beginning of the project. We outline the questions that we were trying to answer and then address each question. We explain the reasons that we found each answer (why people think or behave the way they do) and what the implications of those answers are for the organization. We then outline our recommendations given these results. Our recommendations may sometimes be contentious, but they follow the strategic process that we believe so strongly in using. Our reports typically follow this format:

- •Objectives of this research
- •Major questions we were trying to answer
- •Answer to Question 1
  - ◦ Reasons for findings
  - ◦ Further insight
- •Answer to Question 2
- •Etc.
- •Major implications of findings
- •Recommendations

9

Common Pitfalls
in Market Research

As a professional who has bought and sold market research for over a decade, I am well acquainted with the common pitfalls that occur in this practice. I've seen mistakes by some of my competitors and by some of my clients. Sadly, I've also made a few of my own mistakes along the way. The objective of this chapter is to review some of the major pitfalls to avoid.

Measuring Everything

Early in my career I wanted to please my clients, so when they decided to add another section to a questionnaire, I agreed. I came to regret my decision when the survey came back and we had measured so many things superficially, but we hadn't gone into depth on anything. We could not explore anything to the level that we needed and were unable to provide our clients much insight into their markets. Organizations often want to maximize the money they spend on research, so they throw in as much content as possible into a study. The result is a superficial understanding of many things. This type of research is often not particularly valuable. Sometimes, however, superficiality cannot be helped. No matter how many times you explain that a superficial understanding does not lead to results that can drive strategic decisions, the client somehow knows better. You end up with a questionnaire or a discussion guide that provides a little bit of information about everything possible.

Making Questionnaires Too Long

Another major problem with many surveys is that they are just too long. Long surveys tend to cause respondent boredom and fatigue. Although an organization might want to know every possible attitude toward its product, respondents often do not find such in-depth exploration particularly interesting. After they have answered the fiftieth question about how they think and feel about toothpaste, they are bored. In many cases, respondents have never thought about this category to the level that the questionnaire is written, and that can be fatiguing.

If questionnaires are perceived by respondents as too arduous or too boring, respondents tend to quit them, and the results can be biased. The group that eventually finishes the survey may be a small sample of respondents who are the most interested in the category or are completing the survey for some type of incentive (e.g., money or points for completion). If you only survey the people who are the most interested in a product and you are testing usage and attitudes, you might be surprised to learn that the average survey respondent uses a particular product more often than you expected. The results may not be indicative of usage among the larger population because you have only surveyed those highly involved respondents who completed your questionnaire. The less-involved folks got bored and decided not to finish the survey, so their attitudes and usage will never be known. In addition, if you are testing reactions to a client's potential new service, highly involved respondents should be more interested in that service. Thus, the forecasted purchase of this service will be overestimated.

Insufficient Qualitative Research before Launching Surveys

In the consulting firm where I first learned how to do market research, we were taught to *always* pretest our quantitative surveys with individual interviews. We would design our surveys and then recruit individuals to come into a facility to take the survey in front of us. We would walk through every question with them and determine how they interpreted each question and every response. We would identify if any questions were unclear and if the response categories were appropriate for each question. I can honestly say that all of the surveys we launched using this approach produced the highest-quality data.

I am definitely a proponent of this approach, but sometimes there is not enough time in the schedule to pretest surveys in this way. However, if enough qualitative work has been done to establish a thorough understanding of the product or service, we can use our qualitative research findings to design excellent surveys. There are several reasons why conducting qualitative research, such as individual interviews or focus groups, is important before designing surveys. Excellent qualitative research allows us to become knowledgeable about a category, and we learn the reasons people buy something. We also learn about the major attitudes people have about a brand and its competitors. We also learn how respondents talk about a product and the terminology they use. If we use terminology that is unfamiliar to respondents or refer to thoughts and feelings that don't capture their experiences, people will become frustrated with the survey and stop taking it. Terminology is particularly important. We have done many studies for pharmaceutical companies that are often surprised to learn that patients and physicians will refer to a disease very differently than they do. Even physicians sometimes use incorrect terminology. If we had designed a survey using the pharmaceutical company's terms, there would have been a great deal of confusion on the part of patients and physicians.

Relying on Respondents to Solve a Business Problem

One of the worst uses of market research involves having respondents solve a company's business problems. Expecting respondents to figure out what new products and services a business should offer, asking them to write ad copy, or figuring out how to save a business is a mistake. Respondents are not any more creative or insightful than the rest of us. Great researchers and marketers take market research findings and use them as a tool to find the answer to a business problem. Respondents don't usually give us the answers directly.

One of the most frustrating projects I ever worked on involved an association that wanted to help its members figure out what new services it could offer its customers. This association approached us and asked if we would interview the customers of their members to learn what additional services the association members could offer their customers to make more money. We strongly recommended against using market research for this objective. We were concerned that these customers wouldn't know what else they wanted to buy from these members and might be disinterested in spending more money. The association resisted our advice and decided to forge along with the project. We interviewed several customers and asked them what else they would like to buy from these members. They told us one of two things: either they didn't want to buy anything else or that they couldn't think of anything else for these members to sell them. We were asking too much of them. They couldn't solve the business problems of these members any better than the association.

If you want to use market research to answer these types of strategic questions, the best approach is to put options in front of respondents and get their reactions. Instead of asking respondents what services they want, I advocate putting potential services in front of them. By understanding their reactions to these potential ideas, we can begin to see patterns in what they want. We can identify what they like about each offering and then combine them into a service that they would be likely to buy. Similarly, if you need to understand how to communicate the attributes of a product, put some descriptions in front of respondents and then discern what concepts, words, and phrases they respond positively to in order to revise and refine your communications.

Having Unrealistic Expectations of Market Research

The last major pitfall that we've observed concerns having unrealistic expectations of market research. This pitfall is similar to the previous one, but it goes a little deeper. Some organizations expect market research to be the great panacea. Occasionally I get RFPs (requests for proposals) in which companies state that they want a research study that will: 1) provide the foundation for all their marketing efforts, 2) identify new products and services to launch this year, and 3) give them input for all their communications. I'm being somewhat facetious, but not entirely. Organizations want to maximize their research dollars by cramming as much as they can into one study. This goal is misguided. The result of this type of RFP is research that covers many, many things superficially.

One market research project would be insufficient to achieve one of the objectives above. We could not identify all the new products and services that should be launched this year with one study. Instead, we would conduct several studies and use a variety of methods. First, we would do qualitative research to understand how current products are viewed and to identify the unmet needs that consumers have in this category. Once we've identified these unmet needs, we would create several product concepts and use qualitative research to get reactions to them and to refine them. The final product concepts would then be tested quantitatively to estimate potential customer demand and to determine the appropriate prices. The results would be used to launch new products or services for the organization.

Conclusion

In this book I've talked about the strategic market research approach and the impact it has on organizations. This approach is used at every stage of a research project. It all begins when we think about a strategic question for an organization. At this point, we ask:

- What is the overarching question that the organization needs to answer?

- What are the specific questions that need to be addressed in order to answer this overarching question?

- What are the current hypotheses about the answer to this question?

- What actions will the organization take as a result of knowing this information?

Once we know the answers to these questions, we can design the research project and select the appropriate data collection methods. Qualitative methods are appropriate at the beginning of a project for understanding the many thoughts, feelings, and behaviors of a group of people. We then use quantitative research to measure the things that we unearthed in qualitative work and to test our hypotheses. The specific qualitative and quantitative techniques we use depend on the objectives of our project and the tradeoffs we need to make for the study. Because all research techniques have their advantages and disadvantages, we highly recommend mixed-method designs because they allow you to balance the pros and cons of different research techniques.

Now the real work begins as we delve into our project and try to get the depth we need to answer the strategic question. There are numerous ways to gain insight through qualitative research. One way is to hear more than just what respondents are saying, and another way is to ask the same questions in several different ways to understand the parameters of an answer. Other ways of getting a deep understanding involve probing, testing specific hypotheses, and testing potential scenarios. In general, the goal of qualitative research is to have a different discussion in the last focus group or interview than in the first one. Over time, you will gain a deeper understanding of the issue and will understand it in a different way. Obtaining depth in quantitative research involves some of the same techniques used in qualitative work, such as testing hypotheses and scenarios, but it also involves using skip patterns and exploring issues in detail with specific groups of respondents. It also involves using open-ended response categories and questions.

One way that we go beyond what respondents tell us in qualitative work is to read the nonverbal communications of research respondents. The method that I developed is PERCEIVE. Each letter stands for a major piece of nonverbal communication. "P" stands for proximity, "E" is for expressions, "R" is for relative orientation, "C" is for contact (physical touching), "E" is for eyes, "I" is for individual gestures, "V" is for voice, and "E" stands for existence of adaptors, which are those small, fidgety behaviors that people do when they're stressed or bored. The sum of all these areas of nonverbal communication speaks volumes. When watching a person, I adhere to three rules: 1) watch for individual variations from his or her baseline, 2) watch for variations from the normal situation, and 3) watch for variations expressed toward different people.

Another way of obtaining insight in research projects is to understand the role that emotions play in how people view brands, products, and services. There are several ways that we delve into the emotional lives of our respondents. Before using any specific techniques, we create an atmosphere of comfort and trust, and we respond to people respectfully and with understanding when they express themselves. We also use a variety of techniques such as projection exercises, word associations, collages, stories, and salient memories. We also talk to respondents about their hopes and dreams to understand what role products and services play in their lives.

As our project evolves into quantitative research, we design our surveys to leverage all of the qualitative work we've done up to this point. We analyze numeric data to understand what drives markets. Our goal is to test our hypotheses and to answer specific questions. We use a variety of research designs and statistical analyses to help us. We query our data and test our hypotheses, leading to other questions and further analyses. By approaching our data analysis in this way, we understand what drives a market.

At the end of the road, we interpret the results and make strategic recommendations for an organization. Unfortunately, just repeating the data to the client is not the answer. Interpreting research results is not just about selecting the concept with the highest score or with the greatest percentage of respondents who liked it. It's about looking more deeply into the research results and asking several questions. What are respondents really saying when they give something a high score? The evaluation criteria that consumers use may be different than the ones we use to help an organization. We assess what consumers are telling us, and then what makes sense for a company. For example, when testing a new product, we consider how well this product fits with the brand, how well the company could execute it, and what the company would need to support its launch.

If you conduct, buy, or use market research, I encourage you to use the strategic approach. It will make the difference between collections of data and findings that inspire and change organizations. Good luck in your future research endeavors!

About the Author

DR. ANNE BEALL is President of Beall Research & Training, Inc. She specializes in strategic market research and has held positions at The Boston Consulting Group (BCG) and National Analysts. During her tenure at BCG, Beall directed market research for the Chicago office.

Beall conducts both qualitative and quantitative market research. She specializes in conducting large-scale, complex strategic studies for Fortune 500 companies. She has conducted research on brand positioning and brand equity, determinants of customer loyalty and switching behavior, development of new product concepts, extendibility of brands, launches of new products and services, pricing, and segmentations of consumers and businesses. She has worked in a variety of industries, including food, beverages, telecommunications, insurance, brokerage firms, utilities, package transportation and delivery, retail, schools, hospitals, foundations, furniture, and personal-care products.

Beall has conducted hundreds of in-depth interviews and focus groups across many industries. She specializes in analyzing what respondents say and, more important, what they do not say. She has an unusual sensitivity for people and has created a method for reading nonverbal behavior called PERCEIVE, which can be used to read respondents when they are unable or unwilling to express their thoughts and feelings. She conducts training on this topic for other researchers and for several corporations.

Beall has written book chapters and articles about consumer psychology and marketing. Her revision of her 1995 book *The Psychology of Gender* was published in January 2004. She also published *Reading the Hidden Communications Around You* in 2009.

Beall received her MS, MPhil, and PhD degrees in social psychology from Yale University. In her spare time, she is an amateur photographer and avid runner.

References

Banse, R., & Scherer, K. R. (1996). Acoustic profiles in vocal emotion expression. *Journal of Personality and Social Psychology*, 70, 614–36.

Beall, A. E. (2007). Can a new smile make you look more intelligent and successful? *The Dental Clinics of North America*, 51 (2), 289–97.

Bechara, A. (2004). The role of emotion in decision-making: Evidence from neurological patients with orbitofrontal damage. *Brain and Cognition*, 55, 30–40.

Dovidio, J. F., Kawakami, K., Johnson, C., Johnson, B, & Howard A. (1997). On the nature of prejudice: Automatic and controlled processes. *Journal of Experimental Social Psychology*, 33, 510–40.

Ekman, P. (2003). *Emotions Revealed*. New York: Times Books.

Ekman, P., & Friesen, W. V. (1975). *Unmasking the Face: A Guide to Recognizing Emotions from Facial Clues.* Englewood Cliffs, New Jersey: Prentice-Hall.

Honomichl, J. (2007) 2007 Honomichl Top 50. *Marketing News*, 41 (11), H3–H65

Maestripier, D., Schino, G., Aureli, F. & Troisi, A. (1992). A modest proposal: Displacement activities as an indicator of emotions in primates. *Animal Behavior*, 44, 967-79.

Myers, D. G. (2002). *Social Psychology*, 7th Edition. New York: McGraw-Hill.

Pittam, J. & Scherer, K. R. (1993). Vocal expression and communication of emotion. In M. Lewis & J. Haviland (Eds.), *The Handbook of Emotion* (pp. 185–97). New York: Guilford Press.

Remland, M. S. (2000). *Nonverbal Communication in Everyday Life*. Boston: Houghton Mifflin Company.

Skeeter, S. (2007). *How serious is polling's cell-only problem?* Pew Research Center Publications, February, 4, 2008. http://pewresearch.org/pubs/515/polling-cell-only-problem

Skeeter, S. (2006). *The cell phone challenge to survey research*. Pew Research Center Publications, February, 4, 2008. http://people-press.org/reports/pdf/276.pdf.

"Greg Kot tells us what happened . . . in his well-reported book about music in the Internet Age. . . . Kot understands that it's always entertaining to detail the thrash and roar of a carnivorous dinosaur in its death throes, as small and clever mammals—in this case, music lovers—win the day."

—*The New York Times Book Review*

"[*Ripped*] is the best kind of journalism, even-tempered and provocative, factual and soulful."

—*The Christian Science Monitor*

"Greg Kot's insider access and the chops honed as a music critic give this book a richness that makes it an indispensable survey of the turbulent turn-of-the-century music scene."

—*Chicago Tribune*

"Engaging . . . nimble."

—Michiko Kakutani, *The New York Times*

"Thought-provoking . . . enlightening . . . [a] substantive examination of the chaotic music world."

—*San Francisco Chronicle*

"Informative and entertaining."

—HuffingtonPost.com

"If you're looking for a big-picture guide to music, and how you interact with it, right this second, *Ripped* is a good way to go."

—*Nylon* magazine

"Utterly fascinating, *Ripped* is indispensable for anyone who wants to understand popular music in the twenty-first century."

—*Kirkus Reviews*

"[Kot's] breezy, ████████████ ████████████ ympathetic tone consistently dra███████████████████████ se interested in the intersection███████ ████ and technology."

—*Library Journal*

"Stands out for its sturdily constructed prose and command of up-to-date facts."

—*Publishers Weekly*